S. Hrg. 114–90

THE PRESIDENT'S REQUEST FOR AUTHORIZATION TO USE FORCE AGAINST ISIS: MILITARY AND DIPLOMATIC EFFORTS

HEARING

BEFORE THE

COMMITTEE ON FOREIGN RELATIONS UNITED STATES SENATE

ONE HUNDRED FOURTEENTH CONGRESS

FIRST SESSION

MARCH 11, 2015

Printed for the use of the Committee on Foreign Relations

Available via the World Wide Web: http://www.gpo.gov/fdsys/

U.S. GOVERNMENT PUBLISHING OFFICE

96–801 PDF   WASHINGTON : 2015

For sale by the Superintendent of Documents, U.S. Government Publishing Office
Internet: bookstore.gpo.gov   Phone: toll free (866) 512–1800; DC area (202) 512–1800
Fax: (202) 512–2104   Mail: Stop IDCC, Washington, DC 20402–0001

(II)

CONTENTS

THE PRESIDENT'S REQUEST FOR AUTHORIZATION TO USE FORCE AGAINST ISIS: MILITARY AND DIPLOMATIC EFFORTS

WEDNESDAY, MARCH 11, 2015

U.S. SENATE,
COMMITTEE ON FOREIGN RELATIONS,
Washington, DC.

The committee met, pursuant to notice, at 9:33 a.m., in room 106, Dirksen Senate Office Building, Hon. Bob Corker (chairman of the committee) presiding.

Present: Senators Corker, Risch, Rubio, Johnson, Flake, Gardner, Perdue, Isakson, Paul, Barrasso, Menendez, Boxer, Cardin, Shaheen, Coons, Murphy, Kaine, and Markey.

OPENING STATEMENT OF HON. BOB CORKER, U.S. SENATOR FROM TENNESSEE

The CHAIRMAN. The Foreign Relations Committee will come to order. I want to welcome our distinguished witnesses today, and thank you for taking the time to be here. This is an important topic. We know that each of you has been traveling extensively, and again want to thank you for being with us today to share your insights.

I think everybody on this committee cares first and foremost that we have a policy, a strategy, to deal with ISIS that is in relation to our national interests, that the two are aligned. And I think that is paramount, and what most people in America care about, and certainly everyone on this committee.

Secondarily to that, from my perspective, is the authorization process itself, and yet we find ourselves in an interesting place. The President, which I appreciate, has sent to us an authorization for the use of military force. That was welcomed I think by both sides of the aisle. As we have received that authorization for the use of military force, what we have come to understand is that, and this is not a pejorative statement, it is an observation: we do not know of a single Democrat in Congress—in the United States Senate anyway—that supports that authorization for the use of military force.

On the other hand, the authorization for the use of military force that has been sent up is one that is limited in some ways, both in duration and relative to the activities that the Commander in Chief, through you, can carry out. And so, what that does on this side of the aisle is put Republican Senators in the position of looking at a limited authorization for the use of military force that in some ways ratifies a strategy, especially in Syria, that many people do not believe is effective—one that does not show the commitment necessary to really be successful in the short term.

So I think this hearing today will be very helpful in trying to come together and to understand, number one, that we have a strategy in Syria that is in our national interests, that we have a strategy in Iraq that is in our national interests, and we understand that ISIS obviously is promulgating in many other places.

I was in Baghdad and Erbil 3 weeks ago, and regardless of how we have gotten to where we are today, and I know a lot of things have been said about decisions that have been made along the way, one of the things that jumped out at me, very glaringly, is that in many ways every single thing the United States is doing right now in Iraq, things that I support, I might add, to deal with ISIS, every single thing that we are doing is really inuring to the benefit of Iran. In other words, we are making Iraq a better place for Iran.

No doubt Abadi wants one foot in our country and one foot in Iran, and no doubt he is looking for our assistance, and no doubt he looks to us as a balance. But when you look at the way Iran has permeated the Parliament there, when you look at Suleimani and the fact that he is a celebrity in Iran now and leading the efforts of the Shia militia, it is something that jumps out. And I hope that during today, all of you will be able to illuminate how we should feel about that. Should we care? I know we have had numbers of people getting exercised about the fact that we have Iranian-led Shia militia dealing with ISIS.

Because of the observations that I have made, I am not sure that that should even be an issue. In essence, we are working toward the same end, but I would love to hear your thoughts on that. And what may occur after March 24 in the event there is not an agreement with Iran over the nuclear program, how will that affect how the Shia militia—that is very close in proximity to our own men and women in uniform—how that might affect them.

And in closing, I hope that what you will do today also is to illuminate to us why some of the decisions we know are key. After being in Erbil and Baghdad, I was in Ankara with our Turkish friends. I know a decision memo has been in front of the President for some time relative to an air exclusion zone in Aleppo, and decisions about how we may or may not deal with protecting those that we are training and equipping right now to come in against ISIS. I do not think we have made those decisions yet. And I think to many of us here, what that shows is potentially a lack of commitment, if you will, to really deal with ISIS in a more significant way. That may not be the case, and I hope today during your testimony we will be able to understand more fully the lack of those decisions being made, what that means relative to the overall effort.

So I welcome you here. And I think all three of you have been highly regarded by members of the United States Senate on both sides of the aisle. And we trust your testimony today will be very beneficial to us as we move ahead. And with that, I will turn to our very, very distinguished ranking member, Senator Robert Menendez.

OPENING STATEMENT OF HON. ROBERT MENENDEZ, U.S. SENATOR FROM NEW JERSEY

Senator MENENDEZ. Thank you, Mr. Chairman. Thank you to Secretaries Kerry and Carter and Chairman Dempsey, for being here with us today.

Last December, this committee reported a resolution to authorize the use of military force to counter ISIL. We acted because many of us shared a view then and now that we stood with the President to defeat ISIL, that the 2001 AUMF was not and is not intended to apply to our current engagement in Iraq and Syria. We believed then as now that it is imperative that Congress authorize any further military action against ISIL. It is imperative that we do not shoehorn this conflict into an old AUMF. And it may be convenient, but it is not right. We have an obligation to the families who are sending their children into harm's way to understand our goals, what is achievable and what is not, and ultimately to vote to authorize or not authorize the use of force.

The committee had extensive discussions of many of these issues last year, and the AUMF we passed had a restriction on the deployment of ground troops, allowing for all potential uses that the administration had so far identified, including the use of special operations forces to go after high value ISIL targets, search and rescue of downed pilots, the use of forward air controllers with Iraqi units to better direct coalition airstrikes. It also repealed the 2002 AUMF in Iraq and set a 3-year timeframe for Congress to reconsider the 9/11 AUMF.

What it did not do, and what I think Democrats are not willing to do, is to give this or any other President an open-ended authorization for war, a blank check. And as someone who opposed the 2002 Iraq AUMF, and who has seen the 2001 authorization that I did support go far beyond where anyone would have contemplated, this is the critical question moving forward.

So I look forward to getting some answers from our witnesses that will allow us to move forward in writing and passing an authorization. But we need to know what combat operations may be undertaken by United States troops on the ground in Syria and Iraq. We need to know whether associated forces that come under this agreement could include forces affiliated with ISIL in Libya, Nigeria, or elsewhere. We need to know whether a new administration could revert to relying on the 2001 AUMF in 3 years if this AUMF, if passed, were to expire. And we need to know how long we expect to be there and what our exit strategy will be, what metrics will indicate success, or tell us it is time to bring troops home.

We heard from General Allen 2 weeks ago that under the President's proposed language prohibiting enduring offensive combat forces, that U.S. troops could be deployed for as little as 2 weeks or as long as 2 years before they would trigger the restriction on no enduring offensive operations. On the other hand, General Dempsey said last week that he does not view this language as time restrictive, but as mission specific. So General Dempsey believes the language in this AUMF would allow, for example, United States ground forces to accompany Iraqi forces into Mosul. Clearly, there is a need to define exactly what would be allowed. And it would seem to me that legally there is at least the potential for large numbers of United States troops to be deployed in Iraq and Syria, and maybe beyond, with the authorization as submitted.

So, Mr. Chairman, I look forward to hearing the answers to these and other questions from our distinguished witnesses, and I thank you for this opportunity.

The CHAIRMAN. Absolutely. Thank you for your comments. And, again, we have three outstanding witnesses. We want to welcome you here. As I understand it, Secretary Kerry is going to begin, followed by Secretary Carter, followed by Chairman Dempsey. We are honored that you are here before us. Look forward to your testimony, and I think you all know the drill. If you will, keep it to about 5 minutes if that is possible, and we will ask questions after. Thank you for being here.

STATEMENT OF HON. JOHN F. KERRY, SECRETARY OF STATE, U.S. DEPARTMENT OF STATE, WASHINGTON, DC

Secretary KERRY. Well, Chairman Corker and Ranking Member Menendez, members of the committee, we are pleased to be here. I am pleased to return here, and particularly so in the distinguished company of Defense Secretary Ash Carter and our Chairman of the Joint Chiefs of Staff Marty Dempsey.

From my 29 years of service on this committee, I have nothing but respect for the committee's prerogatives, and particularly the role that it can play on a critical issue like this. We are very simply looking for, as I think both of you, Mr. Chairman, Ranking Member Menendez, have said, the appropriate present-day authorization, not, as you said, Senator Menendez, 2001, but a 2015 statement by the United States Congress about the authority with which we should be able to go after, degrade, and destroy, as the President has said, the group known as ISIL or Daesh.

Now, Mr. Chairman, in our democracy, there are many views about the challenges and the opportunities that we face, and that is appropriate. That is who we are. But I hope we believe that there is an overwhelming consensus that Daesh has to be stopped. Our Nation is strongest, always has been, when we act together. It is a great tradition in this country of foreign policy having a special place, that politics ends at the water's edge, and that we will act on behalf of our Nation without regard to party and ideology.

We simply cannot allow this collection of murderers and thugs to achieve, in their group, their ambition, which includes, by the way, most likely the death or submission of all those who oppose it, the seizure of land, the theft of resources, the incitement of terrorism across the globe, the killing and attacking of people simply for what they believe or for who they are. And the joint resolution that is proposed by the President provides the means for America and its representatives to speak with a single powerful voice at this pivotal hour.

When I came here last time, I mentioned that——

[Disturbance in hearing room.]

VOICE. The American people are speaking out, Secretary Kerry. We are tired of an endless war. We do not want go into war with no——

The CHAIRMAN. The committee will be in order. Look, we appreciate——

VOICE [continuing]. In another endless war and killing of innocent people.

The CHAIRMAN. Okay. If this happens again, I would ask the police to immediately escort people out of the room.

VOICE [continuing]. Creating more terrorism, killing more innocent people.

Secretary KERRY. Killing more innocent people. I wonder how our journalists who were beheaded and a pilot who was fighting for freedom who was burned alive, what they would have to say to their efforts to protect innocent people.

ISIL's momentum has been diminished, Mr. Chairman. It is still picking up supporters in places obviously. We have all observed that. But in the places where we have focused and where we are asking you to focus at this moment in time, it is clear that even while savage attacks continue, there is the beginning of a process to cut off their supply lines, to take out their leaders, to cut off their finances, to reduce the foreign fighters, to counter the messaging that has brought some of those fighters to this effort. But to ensure its defeat, we have to persist until we prevail in the broad-based campaign along multiple lines of effort that have been laid out over the course of the last months.

The President already has statutory authority to act against ISIL, but a clear and formal expression of this Congress' backing at this moment in time would dispel doubt that might exist anywhere that Americans are united in this effort. Approval of this resolution would encourage our friends and our partners in the Middle East. It would further energize the members and prospective members of the global coalition that we have assembled to oppose Daesh. And it would constitute a richly deserved vote of confidence in the men and women of our Armed Forces who are on the front lines prosecuting this effort on our behalf. Your unity would also send an unmistakable message to the leaders of Daesh. They have to understand they cannot divide us. Do not let them. They cannot intimidate us, and they have no hope of defeating us.

The resolution that we have proposed would give the President a clear mandate to prosecute the armed component of this conflict against Daesh and associated persons or forces which we believe is carefully delineated and defined. And while the proposal contains certain limitations that are appropriate in light of the nature of this mission, it provides the flexibility that the President needs to direct a successful military campaign. And that is why the administration did propose a limitation on the use of "enduring offensive ground combat operations." I might add, that was after the committee—then committee chair, Senator Menendez, and the committee moved forward with its language, and we came up here and testified, and responded basically to the dynamics that were presented us within the committee and the Congress itself.

So the proposal also includes no geographic limitation, not because there are plans to take it anywhere, but because it would be a mistake to communicate to ISIL——

[Disturbance in the hearing room.]

VOICE. The United States in the world. The United States is killing innocent civilians——

The CHAIRMAN. I would just remind those in the audience—we live in a country where people have the opportunity to express themselves in democratic ways. We would hope that you would allow this hearing to proceed in an orderly way and respect other citizens' rights to be here and to observe what is happening in a civil manner. I would say that I do not think you are helping your cause. I would say you are hurting your cause, and hopefully you will remain in an appropriate manner. Thank you.

Secretary KERRY. Mr. Chairman, thank you. The point of the no geographic limitation is not that there are any plans or any contemplation. I think the President has been so clear on this. But what a mistake it would be to send a message to Daesh that there are safe havens, that there is somehow just a two-country limitation, so they go off and put their base in a third country, and then we go through months and months of deliberation. Again, we cannot afford that. So that is why there is no limitation.

And, Mr. Chairman, we know that there are groups in the world, affiliated terrorist groups, who aspire to harm the United States, our allies, our partners. Daesh is, however, very distinctive in that because it holds territory, and it will continue if not stopped to seize more because it has financial resources, because of the debilitating impact of its activities in the broader Middle East, because of its pretensions to worldwide leadership, and because there have been culpable and violent deaths of Americans and others.

And I do not need to preview for this committee the full litany of the outrages that are committed by Daesh. But let me just say that just among them, scratching the surface, are atrocities against Syrian Christians and Yazidi religious communities, the crucifixion of children, the sale and enslavement of women and girls, the hideous murder of captives from as near as Jordan and as distant as Japan, and the destruction of irreplaceable cultural and historical sites, the plunder and destruction of cities and towns in which followers of Islam worship and raise their families.

Now, I testified before this committee just a couple of weeks ago regarding our strategy for disrupting and defeating ISIL. That strategy continues to move forward on all fronts. Secretary Carter and General Dempsey will touch on the military elements. But I can say from a diplomatic perspective that the world is strongly united in seeking Daesh's defeat. Our coalition is receiving help from governments throughout and beyond the Middle East, governments that may disagree on other issues, but not about the need to take decisive action against Daesh.

And to date, we have a coalition of some 62 members, including 14 nations that are contributing directly to the operations against Daesh in Iraq or in Syria, 16 of which have committed to help train or otherwise assist Iraqi security forces. Since the coalition came together less than half a year ago, we have stopped ISIL's surge, we have degraded its leadership, we have forced it to change its communications and its movement and its tactics, and heavily damaged its revenue generating oil facilities. And if you have a classified briefing, I think you will get a very good grounding in the progress that is being made to date.

We continue to see progress in governance in Iraq where new leaders are working to strengthen and reform the country's security forces through the purging of incompetent or corrupt officers and the more extensive inclusion of Sunni fighters. In Tikrit right now, there are nearly a thousand Sunni taking part. There is a cross section of engagement.

So, Mr. Chairman, just to respond—move rapidly here.

The CHAIRMAN. We are not moving that rapidly actually.

Secretary KERRY. Well, that is why I am cutting—I am going to cut to the chase.

The CHAIRMAN. Okay, good.

Secretary KERRY. Responding to the threat posed by ISIL is just not a partisan issue, at least it should not be. It is not even a bipartisan issue. It is really a test that transcends political affiliations, and it is a tremendous challenge to the security of our Nation and to the values of our citizens. And so, it is really the kind of challenge that this committee is here to deal with. And my hope is that we will live up to the tradition that we have never failed to meet in the past, that when we had this kind of challenge, the Congress came together, the Senate particularly, I think, in this format. And I am confident that we can do so here again today and in the next few days.

So I am happy to respond to your questions, but first I will turn to Secretary Carter.

[The prepared statement of Secretary Kerry follows:]

PREPARED STATEMENT OF SECRETARY OF STATE JOHN F. KERRY

Chairman Corker and members of the committee, I'm pleased to return here and to do so in the distinguished company of Defense Secretary Ash Carter and General Martin Dempsey, Chairman of the Joint Chiefs.

This panel is looked to for leadership—and justifiably so—on the full range of international issues, but few topics are of such paramount importance as the one that brings us together today. The administration seeks the committee's support and that of the entire Congress for a joint resolution to authorize the use of military force against the terrorist organization known as ISIL.

Mr. Chairman, in our democracy, there are many views about the challenges and opportunities we face, but I hope and believe that there is an overwhelming consensus that ISIL must be stopped. Our Nation is strongest when we act together— and we simply cannot allow this collection of murderers and thugs to achieve its ambitions—which include the death or submission of all who oppose it, the seizure of land, the theft of resources, and the incitement of terrorist acts across the globe.

The joint resolution proposed by the President provides the means for America and its representatives to speak with a single powerful voice at this pivotal hour, when ISIL's momentum has diminished amid signs of fragmentation—but its savage attacks continue. To ensure its defeat, we must persist until we prevail in the broad-based campaign along multiple lines of effort that is now underway.

The President already has statutory authority to act against ISIL, but a clear and formal expression of your backing would dispel any doubt anywhere that Americans are united in this effort. Approval of this resolution would encourage our friends and partners in the Middle East; it would further energize the members and prospective members of the global coalition we have assembled to oppose ISIL; and it would constitute a richly deserved vote of confidence in the men and women of our Armed Forces. Your unity would also send an unmistakable message to the leaders of ISIL—who must understand that they cannot divide us; they cannot intimidate us; and they have no hope of defeating us.

The resolution we have proposed would give the President a clear mandate to prosecute armed conflict against ISIL and associated persons or forces. And while the proposal contains certain limitations that are appropriate in light of the nature of our mission, it provides the flexibility the President needs to direct a successful military campaign.

That is why the administration has proposed a limitation on the use of "enduring offensive ground combat operations." The administration sees no need for U.S. Forces to engage in enduring offensive ground combat operations against ISIL. That is the responsibility of our local partners—a task they are determined and preparing to meet.

The proposal includes no geographic limitation, although we do not anticipate conducting operations against targets in countries other than Iraq and Syria at this time. It would be a mistake to communicate to ISIL that there are safe havens for them outside of Iraq and Syria, by limiting the authorization to specific countries.

Mr. Chairman, we know that there are many terrorist groups in the world that aspire to harm the United States, our friends, and our partners. ISIL is distinctive, however, because it holds territory and will continue—if not stopped—to seize more; because of its financial resources; because of the destabilizing impact of its activities on the broader Middle East; because of its pretentions to worldwide leadership; and because it has already been culpable in the violent death of Americans. I don't need to review for this committee the full litany of outrages committed by ISIL, but I will say that among them are atrocities against the Assyrian Christian and Yazidi religious communities; the crucifixion of children; the sale and enslavement of women and girls; the hideous murder of captives from as near as Jordan and as distant as Japan; the destruction of irreplaceable cultural sites; and the plunder and destruction of cities and towns in which followers of Islam worship, work, and raise their families.

Just 2 weeks ago—as part of our budget presentation—I testified before this committee regarding our strategy for disrupting and defeating ISIL. That strategy continues to move forward on all fronts. Secretary Carter and General Dempsey will touch on the military elements, but I can say—from the diplomatic perspective—that the world is strongly united in seeking ISIL's defeat. Our coalition is receiving help from governments throughout and well beyond the Middle East—governments that may disagree on other issues but not about the need to take decisive action against ISIL. To date, we have assembled a coalition of 62 members, including 14 nations contributing to air operations against ISIL in Iraq or Syria, and 16 which have committed to help train or otherwise assist Iraqi security forces. Since the coalition came together less than half a year ago, we have stopped ISIL's surge, degraded its leadership, forced it to change its communications and tactics, and heavily damaged its revenue-generating oil facilities.

We also continue to see progress on governance in Iraq, where the new leaders are working to strengthen and reform the country's security forces through the purging of incompetent or corrupt officers and the more extensive inclusion of Sunni fighters.

Have no doubt, marginalizing and defeating ISIL in Iraq will be a difficult and time-consuming process. Defeating ISIL in Syria—with Syria's brutal and repressive government—will be even harder and take more time. But the principles at stake in each country are the same and so is our determination. In Syria, as in Iraq, our goal is to support effective and inclusive leadership and a more stable country where violent extremism is no longer a major threat and refugees are able to return home and live normal lives.

Mr. Chairman and members of the committee, I hope that in thinking about this issue, we will all bear in mind the difference between a future in which ISIL is on the rampage, gobbling up land, attracting recruits, and striving to sow terror beyond every boundary—and a future in which that loathsome organization has been defeated on the battlefield, plunged into bankruptcy, and is widely seen on social media and in the court of public opinion as the loser that it is. Between those two futures; there can be only one choice.

Responding to the threat posed by ISIL is obviously not a partisan issue. It is not really even a bipartisan issue. It's a test that transcends political affiliations altogether; it's a tremendous challenge to the security of our Nation, the values of our citizens, and the well-being of friends and allies across the globe; it's the kind of challenge that this committee and our country have never in the past failed to meet—and that I am confident we will embrace today with courage and unity.

I will be pleased to respond to your questions but with your permission, Mr. Chairman, I will yield first to my colleague and friend, Secretary of Defense Ash Carter.

The CHAIRMAN. Thank you. Secretary Carter, thank you.

STATEMENT OF HON. ASHTON B. CARTER, SECRETARY OF DEFENSE, U.S. DEPARTMENT OF DEFENSE, WASHINGTON, DC

Secretary CARTER. Mr. Chairman, Ranking Member Menendez, all the members of the committee, thank you for giving me the opportunity to be with you today on this important subject. Before I begin, I am sure you are all aware that a UH–60 Blackhawk helicopter was involved in an accident last night near Eglin Air Force Base in Florida. We know there were four air crew, Army, from a National Guard Unit in Hammond, LA, and seven marines assigned to Camp Lejeune, NC, on board that helicopter. And I know that with me—our thoughts and prayers are with them and their families as the search and rescue continues.

Just as I know we are all proud to have the finest fighting force the world has ever known. That is why at the end of my first week as Secretary of Defense I traveled to Afghanistan and Kuwait where I thanked our men and women in uniform for their contributions to important missions. And in Kuwait, I talked with our ambassadors and our military leaders in the region about the campaign against ISIL.

The trip confirmed for me that ISIL represents a serious and complex threat, especially in our interconnected and networked world. But it also confirmed to me that the enemy can be defeated, and we will deliver ISIL a lasting defeat. And I am happy to share my thoughts about that campaign with you, but let me turn to the subject of this hearing, which is the authorization for the use of military force.

And in reviewing the President's AUMF as Secretary of Defense, I asked myself two questions. First, does it provide the necessary authority and flexibility to wage our campaign, allowing for a full range of likely military scenarios? And second, will it send the message to the people I am responsible for, our brave men and women in uniform and the civilian personnel who will wage this campaign, that the country is behind them? I believe the President's AUMF does both, and I urge Congress to pass it. And let me explain why I judge that the proposed AUMF gives the authority and flexibility needed to prevail in this campaign.

First, the proposed AUMF takes into account the reality, as Secretary Kerry has noted already, that ISIL is an organization—as an organization is likely to evolve strategically, morphing, rebranding, and associating with other terrorist groups, while continuing to threaten the United States and our allies. Second, the proposed AUMF wisely does not include any geographical restriction because ISIL already shows signs of metastasizing outside of Syria and Iraq.

Third, the President's proposed authorization provides great flexibility and the military means we need as we pursue our strategy with one exception. The proposed AUMF does not authorize long-term, large-scale offensive ground combat operations like those we conducted in Iraq and Afghanistan because our strategy does not call for them. Instead, local forces must provide the enduring presence needed for an enduring victory against ISIL.

And fourth and finally, the proposed AUMF expires in 3 years. I cannot tell you that our campaign to defeat ISIL would be completed in 3 years, but I understand the reason for the proposed sunset provision. It derives from the important principle stemming from the Constitution that makes the grave matter of enacting an authorization for the use of military force a shared responsibility of the President and Congress.

The President's proposed authorization affords the American people the chance to assess our progress in 3 years' time and provide the next President and the Congress the opportunity to reauthorize it if they find it necessary. To me, this is a sensible and principled provision of the AUMF, even though I cannot assure that the counter-ISIL campaign will be completed in 3 years.

Now, in addition to providing the authority and flexibility to wage a successful campaign, I said I had another key consideration as Secretary of Defense, and that is sending the right signals, most importantly to the troops. Passing the proposed AUMF will demonstrate to our personnel that their government stands behind them. And as Secretary Kerry explained, it will also signal to our coalition partners and our adversaries that the United States government has come together to address a serious challenge.

We all took an oath to protect the Nation and its interests, but to do so we must work together. I know everyone on this committee takes the ISIL threat seriously, and President Obama and everyone at this table does as well. We encourage a serious debate, but I urge you to pass the President's AUMF because it provides the necessary authority and flexibility to wage our current campaign, and because it will demonstrate to our men and women in uniform, some of whom are in harm's way right now, that all of us stand unflinchingly behind them.

Thank you, Mr. Chairman.

[The prepared statement of Secretary Carter follows:]

PREPARED STATEMENT OF ASH CARTER

Chairman Corker, Ranking Member Menendez, and members of the committee, as you know, I recently returned from my first trip abroad as Secretary of Defense.

My last stop was in Kuwait, where I thanked our men and women in uniform for their contributions to an important mission and talked with our Ambassadors and military leaders in the region about our campaign against ISIL.

The trip confirmed for me that ISIL represents a serious and complex threat, especially in our interconnected and networked world. But it also confirmed the enemy can be defeated. We will deliver ISIL a lasting defeat.

Let me take a few moments to share with you my view of this fight.

First, defeating ISIL will require a combined U.S. diplomatic and military effort, and I believe DOD's partners in the U.S. Government, at this table, and in the region, are unified and working together effectively. Second, while the 62-member coalition the United States is leading is a great strength, we can—and we will—do a better job leveraging the individual contributions of each member. Third, while we are conducting the current campaign in Iraq and Syria, it has clear ramifications for other parts of the Middle East and other regions of the world. Fourth, ISIL's sophisticated communications strategy, including its use of social media, requires us to be more creative in combating it in the information dimension.

Our counter-ISIL strategy for enduring success calls for U.S. military and coalition forces to conduct a systematic air campaign in Iraq and Syria, and counts on local forces to conduct ground operations. While our program to train and equip vetted elements of the Syrian opposition is just getting off the ground, our strategy is already having effect in Iraq, where America and our coalition partners have helped local forces—the key to a lasting victory against ISIL—seize the initiative.

In reviewing the President's proposed Authorization for the Use of Military Force, as Secretary of Defense, I asked two questions:

First, does it provide the necessary authority and flexibility to wage our current campaign, allowing for a full range of likely military scenarios?

Second, will it send the message to the people I am responsible for—our brave men and women in uniform, and civilian personnel who will wage this campaign—that the country is behind them?

I believe the President's proposed AUMF does both. And I urge this Congress to pass it.

Let me explain why I judge that the proposed AUMF gives the authority and flexibility needed to prevail in this campaign.

First, the proposed AUMF takes into account the reality that ISIL as an organization is likely to evolve strategically . . . morphing, rebranding, and associating with other terrorist groups, while continuing to threaten the United States and our allies.

Second, the proposed AUMF wisely does not include any geographical restriction because ISIL already shows signs of metastasizing outside of Syria and Iraq.

Third, the President's proposed authorization provides great flexibility in the military means we need as we pursue our strategy, with one exception: the proposed AUMF does not authorize long-term, large-scale offensive ground combat operations like those we conducted in Iraq and Afghanistan . . . because our strategy does not call for them. Instead, local forces must provide the enduring presence needed for an enduring victory.

Fourth and finally, the proposed AUMF expires in 3 years. I cannot tell you our campaign to defeat ISIL will be completed in 3 years. But I understand the reason for the proposed sunset provision. It derives from the important principle, stemming from the Constitution, that makes the grave matter of enacting an authorization for the use of military force a shared responsibility of the President and Congress. The President's proposed authorization affords the American people the chance to assess our progress in 3 years' time, and provides the next President and the next Congress the opportunity to reauthorize if they find it necessary. To me, this is a sensible and principled provision of the AUMF, even though I cannot assure that the counter-ISIL campaign will be completed in 3 years.

In addition to providing the authority and flexibility to wage a successful campaign, I said I had another key consideration as Secretary of Defense: sending the right signals, most importantly, to the troops.

Passing the proposed AUMF will demonstrate to our personnel that their government stands behind them. And, as Secretary Kerry explained, it will signal to our coalition partners and to our adversary that the United States Government has come together to address a serious national challenge.

Mr. Chairman, members of the committee, we have all learned lessons—many of them hard won—from the past 13-plus years of war. Our experience informs our strategy, just as I am sure it informs all our opinions on this issue. I know that some worry the proposed authorization places too many limitations on DOD. And I know others are concerned that the authorization does not impose enough constraints. I am confident that the proposed AUMF gives DOD the authority and flexibility required to execute our strategy and stamp out ISIL.

We all want Congress in this important fight. That is why President Obama committed to an ISIL AUMF, even though existing AUMFs provide the necessary legal authority for our ongoing military operations in Iraq and Syria. It is also why the administration has worked closely with members of this committee and the Congress to develop the proposed language before you. And the discussion we are engaging in today helps the American people understand the stakes in this fight, just as our civil deliberation stands in sharp contrast to the discourse of our barbaric and oppressive enemy.

We all took an oath to protect the Nation and its interests. But to do so, we must work together. I know everyone on this committee takes the ISIL threat seriously. President Obama—and everyone at this table—does as well.

We encourage a serious debate. But I urge you to pass the President's AUMF because it provides the necessary authority and flexibility to wage our current campaign. Because it is the best next step in our work together to degrade and defeat ISIL. And because it will demonstrate to our men and women in uniform—some of whom are in harm's way right now—that all of us stand unflinchingly behind them.

STATEMENT OF HON. GENERAL MARTIN DEMPSEY, CHAIRMAN OF THE JOINT CHIEFS OF STAFF, U.S. DEPARTMENT OF DEFENSE, WASHINGTON, DC

General DEMPSEY. Mr. Chairman, Ranking Member, distinguished members of this committee, thank you for the opportunity to appear before you today. Let me begin by adding my personal thoughts and prayers to those of the Secretary of Defense at the loss of the folks on that helicopter, a reminder to us that those who serve put themselves at risk both in training and in combat. And we will work with the services to assure those survivors or, I should say, their family members will be well cared for.

The CHAIRMAN. And if I could, the committee will join in that. Thank you.

General DEMPSEY. Yes, sir. Thank you. I appreciate the opportunity to be here today with Secretary Kerry and Secretary Carter. I just returned yesterday from a trip to the Middle East. I spent a day in Baghdad with Iraqi and U.S. leaders discussing our strategy against ISIL. I also spent a day with my French counterpart and 2,000 of France's sailors and marines aboard the aircraft carrier *Charles de Gaulle* in the Arabian Gulf. Our U.S. Navy aircraft carrier *Carl Vinson* was just off the starboard side. These two great vessels sitting side by side, their combat aircraft, and importantly their crews, are a powerful image of partnership and commitment in this fight. It is actually the solidarity of all of our coalition members that is fundamental to the strength of our campaign against this transregional threat that ISIL represents. The Government of Iraq has a lot of work yet to do with the help of the coalition to ensure ISIL is defeated and, importantly, stays defeated, and that will take time.

I have been consulted on the proposed authorization for the use of military force against ISIL and its associated groups. It is suitable to the campaign as we have presently designed it. We should expect our enemies will continue to adapt their tactics, and we will adapt ours.

Bipartisan support for an AUMF would send an important signal of national support to those who are serving in harm's way conducting this mission. I met with some of them over this past weekend, and they are performing magnificently as you would expect.

I thank you for your commitment to our men and women in uniform, and I look forward to your questions.

The CHAIRMAN. Thank you all for your testimony. And let me just begin with Secretary Carter and Chairman Dempsey. I know that Secretary Kerry mentioned that he feels that currently the AUMF that we have from 2001 and the one from 2002 gives the United States the legal authority in what is now occurring. I just wonder if both of you would answer "yes" or "no" whether you believe that to be the case.

Secretary CARTER. I do, yes.

General DEMPSEY. Yes, Senator.

The CHAIRMAN. Every witness who has come before us on behalf of the administration believes that currently we are operating under a legal premise with what we are doing against ISIS today.

Let me ask you this question, Secretary Carter, Chairman Dempsey. Has there been any indication to the people we are dealing with as part of our coalition or the troops that Congress today is not behind what is happening on the ground with ISIS?

Secretary CARTER. I cannot speak to that, Mr. Chairman. I think that the folks I have talked to of ours do, in fact, believe that the outrages that Secretary Kerry described on the part of ISIL warrant the operation that they are involved in. And, of course, we do not do anything that is not lawful. I am not a lawyer, so I cannot tell you——

The CHAIRMAN. Sure, but they do not—there is no one that you deal with that does not believe that Congress is wholeheartedly behind the effort to deal with ISIS. Is that correct?

Secretary CARTER. I have not talked to people who have the view one way or the other. They know that a hearing like this is going on. I think they know its purpose, and I presume, like me, they welcome a good outcome of it.

The CHAIRMAN. Chairman Dempsey.

General DEMPSEY. I have no data to suggest that they have any doubt about the support of the Congress of the United States or the American people.

The CHAIRMAN. Chairman Dempsey, we have had some great conversations, and I always appreciate your candor. I know you have responded to this in other committees or at least publicly. Should there be any concern by people here that Iran is influencing the outcome against ISIS, has Shia militia on the ground, has some of its own personnel helping command and control? Is that a concern that anyone that cares about U.S. national interests should have?

General DEMPSEY. Yes, of course. There are six things from the military's perspective that concern us about Iranian influence. Four of them are regional, and two of them are global. The four regional concerns are surrogates and proxies, some of which are present in Iraq, in Syria, in Lebanon, and other places in Yemen, weapons trafficking, ballistic missile technologies, and mines that they have developed with the intent to be able to close the Strait of Hormuz if certain circumstances would cause them to do it. And then the two global threats, of course, are their nuclear aspirations, not their nuclear aspirations for a peaceful nuclear program, but for a weapon, which is being dealt with in the negotiations on a diplomatic track. And then cyber is the other global threat they pose.

So Iran's activities across the region and, in the cases of nuclear aspirations and cyber activities, are concerning, of course.

The CHAIRMAN. But as it relates to dealing with Tikrit or Mosul—should we care that Iran's militias and others are involved in helping move ISIS out of those areas, or will help ISIS move out those areas when we begin the Mosul attack?

General DEMPSEY. I think there is general consensus both inside of our own forces and also with the coalition partners with whom I engage that anything anyone does to counter ISIL is, in the main, a good outcome. In other words, the activities of the Iranians to support the Iraqi Security Forces is a positive thing in military terms against ISIL. But we are all concerned about what happens after the drums stop beating and ISIL is defeated, and whether the Government of Iraq will remain on a path to provide an inclusive government for all of the various groups within it. We are very concerned about that.

The CHAIRMAN. And so, the concern is that once we hit that witching hour, if you will, when it appears that ISIS definitely is toward its end, all of a sudden the Shia militias and others would potentially turn on our own military, and other very negative things could occur at that time.

General DEMPSEY. We have no indications that they intend to turn on us, but what we are watching carefully is whether the militias that call themselves the popular mobilization forces, whether when they recapture lost territory, whether they engage in acts of retribution and ethnic cleansing. There is no indication that that is a widespread event at this point, but we are watching closely.

The CHAIRMAN. So if we could move to Syria, I know we talked a little bit about this. But this is, again, a term I think even the administration has begun to utilize themselves. It would appear that in Syria we are sort of in a containment mode, that we are really not taking aggressive steps to turn the tide there. We are obviously involved in some aerial attacks, but that it is more of a containment mode. When we say "Iraq first," Syria is more containment.

We have a train and equip program right now, and I wonder if you could talk to us about two major decisions. One would be if we are going to train and equip folks in other countries that are being trained against ISIS—I know there has been an alleged "other" program that is against Assad himself. But if we are going to have an overt program that is going to deal with ISIS, I would assume that we would consider it only moral that if we are going to train them in other countries and bring them in, that we would supply air power and other support to protect them, especially from Assad's barrel bombs.

I know that Senator Graham may have asked a question about whether this AUMF itself provides that legal authority. And I would just like to ask you: does the AUMF that the President has sent forth provide the legal authority for our military to protect those that we are training in other places against ISIS to protect them against Assad? In other words, take Assad on? And I would also like for you to, if you would, talk to us a little bit about why we have not yet agreed to the air exclusion zone that Turkey has asked us to approve that would more fully bring them in on the ground in Syria and actually get something much more positive occurring, at least as it relates to having some ground effort there.

General DEMPSEY. I take it, Senator—you are looking straight at me, so I assume the question is for me.

The CHAIRMAN. Yes.

General DEMPSEY. So let me just briefly describe the way militarily we characterize our campaign against ISIL in Iraq and in Syria. I would not say that our goal is simply to contain ISIL inside of Syria, but rather we have got at this point militarily a main effort and a supporting effort. Our main effort is in Iraq because we have a credible ground partner for whom we supply this air power to distribute it and to degrade and eventually defeat ISIL inside of Iraq. We do not have that credible partner inside of Syria yet. We are taking steps to build that partner.

In the meantime, we are attacking ISIL where we can using ISAR and close air support, both U.S. and some coalition partners, and it is intended to disrupt their activities so that they cannot complement each other. It was formally before we began this effort that ISIL could transit freely across that Syrian and Iraqi border and reinforce efforts on both sides. They are no longer able to do that. They are isolated and degraded in Syria while we conduct our main effort inside of Iraq.

To your other question about whether the AUMF provides legal authority to protect the new Syrian forces as we have called them, the answer to that is no. We have not—the administration has not added a Syrian regime or an Assad component to the AUMF, although we are in active discussions within the interagency about what support we would supply once the new Syrian forces are fielded. Now, militarily there is a very pragmatic reason. You mentioned the moral obligation, I suppose. Let me not speak to that, but rather let me speak to the——

The CHAIRMAN. Well, if I could, Congress has approved a significant amount of money to train and equip people to go against ISIS, and yet we know Assad will barrel bomb them in all likelihood, or at least members of their——

General DEMPSEY. Right.

The CHAIRMAN. So the President has actually sent us an AUMF that does not allow us to protect them against what we know they will be facing down the road. That, to me, is somewhat odd and does not seem congruent, if you will, with previous steps relative to train and equip. Can you understand why?

General DEMPSEY. No, I understand completely, and I am not discounting the moral obligation. I am rather suggesting that—I am giving you military advice under Article 1 responsibility. And militarily, there is a very pragmatic reason to support them, and that is we are not going to be able to recruit men into that force unless we agree to support them at some level.

The CHAIRMAN. So militarily, I know we have had a pretty good crop that have signed up on the front end, or at least that is my understanding, but we cannot recruit more if we are not going to protect them. And yet the AUMF that we have before us does not allow us to protect them. Is that clearly what you are saying?

General DEMPSEY. We are under active discussion about whether and how to support them, and part of that discussion is the legal authority to do so. And I would defer to those with that expertise.

The CHAIRMAN. And I know I am way over, but the air exclusion zone, what is keeping us from those types of——

General DEMPSEY. Yes. We have been in two rounds of discussions with our Turkish counterparts about that, and we are continuing to develop that option should it be asked for.

The CHAIRMAN. Senator Menendez.

Senator MENENDEZ. Thank you, Mr. Chairman. Senator Boxer is the ranking member on the Environment and Public Works and had to go be part of that hearing. So I ask that her statement be included in the record.

[EDITOR'S NOTE.—Senator Boxer's prepared statement can be found in the "Additional Material Submitted for the Record" section at the end of this hearing.]

Senator MENENDEZ. And I have heard all of you several times refer to "no geographic limitation." And so, for the purposes of the record, let it reflect that the AUMF that was passed out last year that Democrats put together has no geographic limitations, so I think there is—although there was a subject of debate. Nonetheless, it came to a conclusion to have no geographic limitations. So to that extent, you know, I know you have all raised it, and I want to deal with it.

Let me ask you, General Dempsey, is it fair to say that for Iran-sponsored Shia militias in Iraq, fighting ISIL is definitely their immediate interest. But would it also be fair to say they have other designs beyond that?

General DEMPSEY. It would be fair to say that that has not become evident, but it is of great concern to us who have served in Iraq since 2003. Iran is not a new entrant into the crucible of Iraq. They have been there since 2004. And in some cases, their economic influence in other ways has contributed to the future of Iraq, and in other ways it has absolutely been disruptive to the inclusiveness or the potential for an inclusive governance. So, I mean, believe me, I share your concerns, and we are watching carefully.

The Tikrit operation will be a strategic inflection point one way or the other in terms of easing our concerns or increasing them.

Senator MENENDEZ. Well, I know that Suleimani is a cause celebre these days there, so I would like to believe that it is only to fight ISIL. But I do not believe that their purposes at the end of the day—we have different goals as it relates to Iraq, both in the short term as it relates to ISIL, and then in the long term of a Democratic multiethnic government. So it is a continuing concern.

Now, Chairman Dempsey, you said in your remarks, and I do not have a copy of your statement, so correct me if I am wrong here. Something to the extent that the authorization as proposed by the administration basically or substantially, I think was the word, deals with our campaign as we have presently devised it. Is that a fair statement?

General DEMPSEY. That is a fair statement, Senator.

Senator MENENDEZ. Does it also deal with a campaign that may alter more than you have presently devised it?

General DEMPSEY. It deals with the campaign as presently designed, and has statements in there—I do not know which part of it you might be reacting to.

Senator MENENDEZ. Well, let me perfect my question. If, in fact, your campaign as presently designed needs to morph, change, to the realities of what is happening, do you believe the authorization will allow you to do that?

General DEMPSEY. Yes, I do, and that is because as most of us who have both studied and served against these kind of threats over the past now almost 14 years, we believe that the primary way you defeat these groups is by, with, and through partners in the region, and through sustainment of a broad coalition. And that the U.S. Forces involved should principally be enabling, not necessarily leading the effort, although the AUMF does provide—— well, first of all, I will always go back to the Commander in Chief through Secretary of Defense and recommend whatever I think is necessary to accomplish the task. But as I presently conceive—as we presently conceive of this threat and how to defeat it, this AUMF is adequate to the task.

Senator MENENDEZ. Well, and I appreciate that answer because it underlies the challenge that members of the committee have in getting to the right point, to support the President, this and any future one, to degrade and defeat ISIL, and at the same time not to provide the open-endedness so that if, in fact, it meets your present criteria, but you believe it has the wherewithal to meet a future criteria that may morph, that is the essence of the challenge.

And so, last week before the Armed Services Committee, General Dempsey, you, in response to questions, said that your view of what no enduring offensive combat operations would mean would be mission specific. Is that fair to say?

General DEMPSEY. Yes, and I also said that it was—it not a doctrinal term. There is no word "enduring" in military doctrine, but it is a statement of the Commander in Chief's intent.

Senator MENENDEZ. Right. And we all know that it may be the intent of someone not to have any large-scale or long-term offensive combat troops, but that intention can honestly change along the way. And so, that is part of our challenge here.

General Allen testified before this committee last week when we asked him what does no enduring offensive combat operations means to you, and he said, well, that could mean as long as 2 weeks or 2 years. And considering his experience, it was not an insignificant statement. So, Secretary Carter, what does it mean to you as ultimately the Secretary of Defense who oversees all of the armed forces under your Department, of course under the President's command? What does "no enduring offensive combat operations" mean to you?

Secretary CARTER. There are two ingredients to this, the how and the when. And the AUMF as proposed is, as I noted, provides for a wide range of activities to defeat ISIL, but it has one significant limitation, which is the one you referred to, which essentially it does not authorize the kind of campaign that we conducted in Iraq and Afghanistan. That is not what we foresee as necessary for the defeat of ISIL, so it meets my objective of having necessary flexibility, but there is that limitation. That is what is written in, and that is what the meaning of those words is.

As regards to the 3-year limit, as I indicated, that is not based on an assessment of how long the campaign will take. That is based upon how our system works here at home, and it does not have anything to——

Senator MENENDEZ. And I appreciate that, and that is what we did in our authorization. But even without an Iraq or Afghanistan-sized commitment still can commit thousands of troops for a long period of time, and so it may not be the size of Afghanistan or Iraq. So that is part of our challenge.

Two very quick final questions. Secretary Kerry, one of the criticisms of the President's proposed AUMF is that it does not make clear that it is, in fact, this AUMF and not the 2001 AUMF that governs this conflict. If we passed an ISIL-specific AUMF, would the administration have any objection to specifically saying that the ISIL AUMF supersedes any preceding authorization for the use of military force in this engagement?

Secretary KERRY. Senator, only if it was absolutely clear that there was no limitation whatsoever with respect to the other activities authorized by the 2001 AUMF, because that is the principal authorization with respect to al-Qaeda and other efforts. So the

President has made it clear that if the Congress passes an authorization specifically, that is what he will rely on with respect to ISIS.

Senator MENENDEZ. And if that is the case, there is no reason not to have language that says that this is only an authorization.

Secretary KERRY. As long as it is clear that——

Senator MENENDEZ. ISIS specific.

Secretary KERRY. As long as it is clear it does not reach any of the other activities authorized by the 2001, correct.

Senator MENENDEZ. Finally, Secretary Carter, over the weekend, Boko Haram in Nigeria declared its allegiance to ISIL. Would Boko Haram be considered a legitimate target under the language of the President's proposed authorization?

Secretary CARTER. The language of the proposed authorization anticipates, as I indicated, the possibility of other groups aligned with ISIL. And what the text means is that the AUMF would cover such groups that associate with or fight alongside if they also have the intent of threatening Americans. So both of those tests would be applied under the proposed AUMF by——

Senator MENENDEZ. Just saying that with what you have— swearing allegiance will be enough then.

Secretary CARTER. No, it is not enough. It also has to be a threat to Americans.

Senator MENENDEZ. Okay.

Secretary CARTER. That is what the language says. It is says "associated with," et cetera, ISIL and threatening Americans.

Senator MENENDEZ. Thank you, Mr. Chairman.

The CHAIRMAN. Thank you. Senator Rubio.

Senator RUBIO. Thank you. At the outset, I want to thank you all as well for recognizing what happened this morning—last night in my home State of Florida. It is a reminder that the dangers to our service men and women face is not just when they are deployed, but it is inherently dangerous work even in their training. And so, our thoughts and prayers go out to them, and to their families, and loved ones.

Secretary Carter, I wanted to begin by asking you about Iran. Iran's goal is to become the regional—most dominant regional power. Is that accurate?

Secretary CARTER. I am sorry, Iran's?

Senator RUBIO. Iran's goal is to become the regional hegemony——

Secretary CARTER. Probably true, yes.

Senator RUBIO. And in that realm, they see American military presence in the region as a threat or an impediment to that goal, correct?

Secretary CARTER. Probably to the achievement of some of their goals, yes.

Senator RUBIO. And certainly they are never excited to see additional American troops present anywhere in the Middle East. That is a fair statement.

Secretary CARTER. I cannot tell what excites them. I cannot imagine that our bombing ISIL is unwelcome to them, but I do not know that because I do not know what they are thinking.

Senator RUBIO. Well, bombing ISIL is unwelcome to them. General Dempsey, you agree the Iranians are not fans of U.S. military presence in the Middle East.

General DEMPSEY. I think they have the same suspicion about us that we have of them.

Senator RUBIO. But in general, they are not—when they see us in the region, they are not necessarily fans of U.S. military deployments anywhere in the Middle East.

General DEMPSEY. No, I would not think so.

Senator RUBIO. Okay. Well, that is why I want to turn to you, Secretary Kerry. I believe that much of our strategy with regards to ISIS is being driven by a desire not to upset Iran so that they do not want walk away from the negotiating table on the deal that you are working on. Tell me why I am wrong.

Secretary KERRY. Because the facts completely contradict that, but I am not at liberty to discuss all of them here for a lot of different reasons. In a classified session I could, but at this delicate stage of the negotiations, I am not sure that is advisable.

Senator RUBIO. So are you——

Secretary KERRY. The fact is, let me just——

Senator RUBIO. Well, but for the record, can you state that Iran's feelings about our military presence in the region and the fact that they would be upset if we increase military personnel on the ground——

Secretary KERRY. Senator, let me——

Senator RUBIO [continuing]. Would increase—targeting, for example, Assad and Syria. Could you tell me today that under no circumstances is how Iran would react to an increase of U.S. military action against ISIS, because as we heard from Secretary Carter, they are not fans of us bombing ISIS because it involves our presence in the region. Are you telling me that that is a nonfactor in terms of how it would impact the negotiations, or is that something you cannot discuss in this setting?

Secretary KERRY. They would welcome our bombing additionally ISIS actually. They want us to destroy ISIS. They want to destroy ISIS. ISIS is a threat to them. It is a threat to the region. And I think you are misreading it if you think that there is not a mutual interest with respect to Daesh between every country in the region.

Senator RUBIO. So they are supportive of more ground—if the U.S. sent more military personnel into Iraq as trainers, advisers, logistical support, they would support that? Iran would support that?

Secretary KERRY. Well, they are not going to come out and openly support it, and they obviously would be nervous about it, but they are not going to object if that it is what it is. But the point is you have bigger problems than that with that particular scenario because the Shia militia within Iran might have something to say about it. Mukhtar Al Sadr, and Hadi al-Amiri, other people might obviously react very adversely to that.

But what is important, Senator, with respect to your question is to understand this, and I think this has been misread by a lot of people up here on the Hill to be honest with you. There is no grand bargain being discussed here in the context of this negotiation. This is about a nuclear weapon potential. That is it. And the President has made it completely clear they will not get a nuclear weapon.

Now, the presumption by a lot of people up on the Hill here has been that we somehow are not aware of that goal even as we negotiate that goal. Our negotiation is calculated to make sure they cannot get a nuclear weapon, and it is really almost insulting that the presumption here is that we are going to negotiate something that allows them to get a nuclear weapon.

Senator RUBIO. Well, I have not discussed about the nuclear weapon. What I have—and I am not saying there is a grand bargain. What I am saying is that I believe that our military strategy towards ISIS is influenced by our desire not to cross red lines that the Iranians have about U.S. military presence in the region.

Secretary KERRY. Not in the least, no. Absolutely not in the least.

Senator RUBIO. Okay.

Secretary KERRY. There is no consideration whatsoever as to how they or anybody else feels. We will do what is necessary in conjunction with our coalition—remember we have 62 countries, including five——

Senator RUBIO. Okay. Well, I want to talk about the coalition.

Secretary KERRY [continuing]. Five Sunni countries that for the first time ever are engaged in military action in another country in the region.

Senator RUBIO. And I want to touch on that point because General Dempsey a moment ago outlined the need to have a broad coalition, and I imagine it involves these Sunni countries, for example, the Jordanians, the Saudis, the UAE, and others. These are also countries, by the way, that are deeply concerned about Iran, and they feel—is it not right that they feel that we have kept them in the dark about our negotiations with Iran? In essence, the way we have proceeded with our negotiations in Iran have impacted our trust level with these critical allies in this coalition? Is that accurate?

Secretary KERRY. Senator, that actually is flat wrong also. Flat wrong.

Senator RUBIO. They said so——

Secretary KERRY. Just it is flat wrong. I just came back from a meeting in the Gulf in Riyadh. I met with King Salman, who completely supported what we are doing. I met with all of the GCC members. They all sat around the table, and they all articulated their support for what we are doing, and they believe we are better off trying to prevent them from getting a bomb diplomatically first, providing, of course, that it actually prevents them from getting that bomb. That is the test of this. And a whole bunch of people are trying to give this a grade before the test has even been taken.

Senator RUBIO. So you are saying here today that our allies in the region, our Sunni allies, the Saudis, the UAE, the Egyptians, and others, are perfectly comfortable with where the negotiations stand at this moment.

Secretary KERRY. I did not say that. I did not say that. They are not perfectly comfortable. They are nervous. They are apprehensive. Of course they are. They want to make sure that, in fact, just as Members of Congress want to make sure, that the deal that is struck, if one can be struck now, will, in fact, prevent them from getting a weapon.

Senator RUBIO. Have you shared with them the details of where it stands right now?

Secretary KERRY. We have shared considerable details with them, absolutely.

Senator RUBIO. And are they apprehensive about that, or are they comfortable with what you shared with them?

Secretary KERRY. They are comfortable with what we shared with them, and Saud al-Faisal, the senior Foreign Minister in the world, I might add, publicly sat with me at a press conference in which he articulated their support for what we are doing.

Senator RUBIO. Okay. General Dempsey, I want to ask you because we talked about this a moment ago. Part of what is happening here is a second concentric circle that ISIS is pursuing beyond its core in Syria and Iraq, and we have seen that emerge in Libya. We are starting to signs of it emerge in Afghanistan. First, if you can comment about what ISIS, or if any of you could comment, about what we are seeing with ISIS with regard to the competition between them, and al-Qaeda, and the Taliban to absorb groups in Afghanistan. And second, how does this AUMF that is proposed before us today allow us to form a strategy that allows us to deal with that second ring of threats of ISIS absorbing other groups in the region?

General DEMPSEY. The TTP is notably that splinter group of the Taliban, who has rebranded themselves to the ISIL ideology. And the—to answer your question on the AUMF, the AUMF would give me the authority to make recommendations to the Commander in Chief how to deal with ISIL wherever it shows up if the two conditions that the SecDef mentioned exists, number one, that they have affiliated themselves with the ideology, but number two, that they demonstrate an intent to threaten U.S. interests either regionally or globally.

Senator RUBIO. And just my last point here. In Afghanistan, we still have a significant presence of service men and women among other Americans, and much more so than in other parts of the world where they are now getting groups to align themselves. The growth of an ISIS affiliate and/or pledged group in Afghanistan could potentially pose a significant threat to American personnel in Afghanistan potentially.

General DEMPSEY. It will initially pose a threat to the government of Afghanistan, and could over time pose a threat to us.

The CHAIRMAN. Senator Cardin.

Senator CARDIN. Well, thank you very much, Mr. Chairman, and I thank the three of you for your incredible service to our country. We very much appreciate it during this extremely challenging time.

First, let me say I supported the use of force resolution that was reported from this committee in the last Congress, as did every Democrat. And as I was listening to Secretary Carter explain the objectives of and authorization for the use of military force and thought about what we have recommended, it satisfied, I think, every one of your concerns.

And I was somewhat surprised because I think some Republicans were reluctant to support a use of force in the last Congress because the administration had not come forward with a request. In fact, that was said by many of my Republican colleagues. So I was somewhat surprised that the administration did not bring a resolution that was more consistent with what we developed in the last Congress, and would have accomplished every one of the objectives that Secretary Carter pointed out.

So let me bring up three concerns in the time I have. Some have already been raised, but I will try to get through as much of this as possible. First, dealing with the 2001 authorization and why there is nothing included in your request that deals with the 2001 authorization. Secondly, to deal with the interpretation of "enduring offensive ground combat operations." And third, how you will determine associated forces. All three give me concern.

In regards to the 2001 authorization, as it has been pointed out, that was an authorization passed rather easily by Congress to go after those that were responsible for the attack of our country on September 11, 2001. That is what the resolution says. I think many of us are surprised that that authorization could be used today against ISIS in Syria.

The 2001 authorization is now the longest running use of force in American history, 4 years longer than the Vietnam War, 8 years longer than the Revolutionary War, 10 years longer than World War II. About one-third of the authorizations for use of military force passed by Congress have included limitations of time, so that is not an unusual provision to be placed in a resolution. As Secretary Carter pointed out, the circumstances can change and it is important that Congress and the administration speak with a united voice.

And, Secretary Carter, I was very impressed by your comments about the constitutional responsibilities between Congress and the administration, and you fully understand a 3-year sunset on the ISIS-specific authorization for the use of force. And quoting from your statement, "To me, this is a sensible and principled provision of the AUMF, even though I cannot assure that the counter-ISIL campaign will be completed in 3 years."

So Senator Murphy and I have introduced a bill that would limit the 2001 authorization to the same 3-year provision that you have in the ISIS-specific resolution. And if Congress choses to include a 3-year sunset on the 2001 authorization, would it be your view that that would be a sensible and principled provision for Congress to include, even though you could not assure that the military operation against those responsible for the attack on our country on September 11, 2001 can be completed in that time, that it would be up to the next administration to come back, as it would in the ISIS campaign?

Secretary CARTER. Senator, thank you for that. I cannot give you a clear answer to that question, and let me say why. The 2001 authorization on the use of military force covered al-Qaeda and its successive generations, which have now extended for 14 years. There is still an al-Qaeda in the Arabian Peninsula. They call themselves that, and they intend to attack this country, and we need to protect ourselves. And we need the authority to protect ourselves.

Senator CARDIN. Is that not also true of ISIS?

Secretary CARTER. Well, there is a difference. There is now a 14-year history of the tenacity of al-Qaeda and its offshoots and their intent to attack our country. And I think you have to take that into account about whether it makes sense to put a sunset on that one. This one that we are embarking on with ISIL is a new campaign, a new group.

And so, as I said in my statement, I respect the desire to have a sunset clause that does not derive from any characteristic of the campaign that I know of yet that would predict that it will wrap up within 3 years. But I think we have history in the case of al-Qaeda that it has endured—it has lasted quite a long time. And I think that ought to inform whether a sunset for the authorities contained in the AUMF makes sense.

Senator CARDIN. Mr. Secretary, if this is a new campaign, I do not understand how you can use a 2001 authorization to justify the use of force. I think you cannot have it both ways. So I do not understand the distinction there when you are saying it is a new campaign, we do not know what is going on, and yet we still can use a 2001 authorization that was specific against the attack on our country.

Secretary CARTER. Well, I think maybe another way of getting at your question, Senator, is the President has indicated a desire and a willingness to revisit the 2001——

Senator CARDIN. And we are trying to help that along.

Secretary CARTER [continuing]. AUMF, which I also think makes sense in view of what you have said. It has been 14 years. The only thing that I would say, and the only reason I am hesitating here is that we have to protect ourselves against al-Qaeda and its successors.

Senator CARDIN. And the Congress——

Secretary CARTER. Those guys are still out there 14 years after 9/11.

Senator CARDIN. And our Congress will meet again and can always take up, as they will, I assume, if this resolution was passed in the next Congress with the next administration. I want to just get one more question in on the enduring offensive ground combat troops. I looked at my app on my phone here to get a definition of what "enduring" is, and it came up as "lasting, permanent."

So would you tell me why the term "enduring offensive ground combat operations" could not be interpreted to include operations such as our military operations in Iraq and Afghanistan since we did not intend our troops to be there on a permanent basis, that instead we were liberating, we were not offensive? Why could you or the administration not interpret that language to include a ground campaign similar to what we saw in Iraq?

Secretary CARTER. I will let Senator Kerry. I am not a lawyer, but the interpretation that I gave to that phrase is the interpretation that those who drafted the AUMF make of it. And it is intended in the first instance clearly to rule out the kind of campaign we waged in Iraq and Afghanistan because we do not foresee that kind of campaign as necessary. And that is one of the things that those words are supposed to cover. Let me ask Secretary Kerry to add to that.

Secretary KERRY. Well, I think the President, Senator, has been particularly clear about this. And there is a huge distinction between the kinds of operations that were conducted in Afghanistan and Iraq where clearly we committed a very significant number of troops for a long period of time to offensive actions on the ground. The President has ruled that out, and what he has done is, I think, offered you confining definitions that provide the limitations here. And I think the English language provides them also frankly.

I do not happen to agree with General Allen's comment here about 2 weeks to 2 years. I do not think anybody contemplates years or a year. That is not in the thinking of the President nor any of the considerations he has said. What he has thought of only, and what General Dempsey has been particularly clear about it, is not giving up the option under some particular circumstances where you might want somebody on a special forces nature or embedded nature somehow to be accompanying people, to be assisting in some way.

I do not want to go into all the parameters of that, but I think it has been very clear how limited it is, or an effort to protect or defend U.S. personnel or citizens, which is momentary, an effort to rescue people in some particular instance. Perhaps a specific targeted operation against Daesh leadership for instance. Perhaps intelligence collection and sharing.

I mean, there is a range that has been laid out, but the whole purpose here is to kind of have a concept that is well understood that is extremely limited, but not so limiting that our military cannot do what it needs to do in some situations to protect America's interests or American personnel. But it is not contemplating years, not even months to my knowledge. What it would contemplate is some current operation along the lines that I just described.

Senator CARDIN. I would just point out that the language we used in 2001—I think most of us would not have thought it would be used today. This authorization goes to the next administration, so the next administration would have the authority and may have a totally different view on that.

Secretary KERRY. It may indeed, Senator, which is precisely why President Obama said I am going to put it in the 3-year range, and he specifically thought that through. He said, you know, I do not want the new President to come in and face the kind of choice that I faced on my desk day one, which had to be made within 30 days with respect to Afghanistan. So he gave it the distance of the year to allow the administration to get its people in place, to evaluate and make a decision.

But most importantly, this is where there is a broadly accepted and absolutely clear congressional responsibility. Congress will step in. You will have the authority. I mean, I would think you would be welcoming this opportunity to double check the next administration, to be able to make sure this is accomplishing the precise goals you want. In fact, you know, I would think it would be undebated by Congress in that respect, although I understand there are principles where people say, you know, we do not want any limitations at all.

But this certainly fits within the capacity to get a major vote out of Congress. And may I say to everybody, you know, that is something else you have got to think about here. When I testified in December and when I testified 2 weeks ago, I think I made it clear that our interests are best served if there is a very powerful vote in support of this. We do not have a message of America's commitment and of our willingness to stay at it and get the job done if this is, you know, a marginal vote in the Congress.

The CHAIRMAN. Thank you. We do welcome this opportunity—we also welcome the opportunity to weigh in on any final Iran deal and look forward to that. And with that, Senator Johnson.

Senator JOHNSON. Words matter, and I know we are here really discussing specific language on authorization for the use of military force, but this is puzzling. Secretary Kerry, you said this authorization needs to be extremely limited, but show the commitment of the United States. I do not see how you reconcile those two terms. There have been an awful lot of loose statements here.

Let us talk about the joint resolution passed on September 18, 2001, and why the current activity is tenuously connected to that at best. That joint resolution was to authorize the use of the United States Armed Forces against those responsible for the recent attacks launched against the United States specifically. It said that "The President is authorized to use all necessary and appropriate force against those nations, organizations, or persons he determines planned, authorized, committed, or aided the terrorist attacks that occurred on September 11, 2001, or harbored such organizations or persons in order to prevent any future attacks of international terrorism against the United States by such nations, organizations, or persons." I did not hear anything about successor organizations.

So, again, I am puzzled by the fact that the administration is firmly of the view that they already have statutory authority to conduct what they are conducting, and I guess there is really nobody pushing back that hard on that. But now we are talking about a new authorization, and I am puzzled by the fact that any Commander in Chief, if they already believe they have the authority to do what is being conducted, why they would want to limit that in any way, shape, or form, particularly when, Secretary Kerry, you said you want to dispel any doubt, and send an unmistakable message.

Let me just read two other authorizations. This is the authorization we are discussing because we are talking about it, but let us talk about the specific words. It says "The President is authorized, subject to the limitations in Subsection (c), to use the Armed Forces of the United States as the President determines to be necessary and appropriate against ISIL or associated persons or forces as defined in Section 5." Man, this sounds like a contract. (C), limitations. "The authority granted in Subsection (a) does not authorize the use of United States Armed Forces in enduring offensive ground combat operations." Okay, that is not a real dispelling of doubt. Duration of, "this authorization for the use of military force shall terminate three years after the date of the enactment of this joint resolution, unless reauthorized." I do not know. I am not seeing that sending an unmistakable message.

Let me read you one other authorization. This was passed on December 8, 1941. "The President is hereby authorized and directed to employ the entire naval and military force of the United States and the resources of the Government to carry on war against the Imperial Government of Japan; and, to bring the conflict to a successful termination, all of the resources of the country are hereby pledged by the Congress of the United States."

Now, if we are discussing language to dispel all doubt, to send an unmistakable message, General Dempsey, which authorization, as a military man, would you want to have at your back?

General DEMPSEY. Senator, I am not going to compare something from 1941, which is a state-on-state global conflict, to a conflict with a non-state actor. I was consulted on this AUMF.

Senator JOHNSON. Secretary Carter, it has always puzzled me why anybody would want to pick a fight with the United States. Why is ISIS putting out on videotape the barbaric beheadings of Americans and of other Westerners? Why would they do that? Why would anybody want to pick a fight with the United States?

Secretary CARTER. Senator, I can only say and read as you can hear and read what they say, which is that they intend to create an Islamic state, and they regard us and our friends and allies as standing in the way of that. And, therefore, they have shown their willingness to attack Americans and attack our allies and interests.

Senator JOHNSON. But, again, I would never pick a fight with Chairman Dempsey's military. So the only way I would pick that fight is——

Secretary CARTER. Well, as I think I said in my statement, we will defeat them.

Senator JOHNSON. The only way I would pick that fight is if I really did not think America would be serious about coming back to defeat me, to try and accomplish that goal that President Obama established.

I do want to talk a little bit about the current ground forces allied against ISIS. General Dempsey, do we know basically what the force structure is? How many Iraqi Security Forces are there? How many Kurds? How many in the Shia militias sponsored by Iran? What is the current force structure of boots on the ground?

General DEMPSEY. I have to get back to you for the record on the exact number, Senator.

[EDITOR'S NOTE.—The information supplied to Senator Johnson was classified.]

Senator JOHNSON. Well, I am happy to get ballpark figures.

General DEMPSEY. Okay. Well, let us talk about the Tikrit operation for example. There are approximately a thousand Sunni tribal folks. There is one brigade of the Iraqi Security Forces, which numbers approximately 3,000, a couple hundred of their CTS, their counterterrorist service. Those are the MOD-sponsored forces. And there are approximately 20,000 of the popular mobilization forces, which are the Shia militia.

Senator JOHNSON. So the Shia militia dramatically outnumber the Iraqi Security Forces in this?

General DEMPSEY. They do.

Senator JOHNSON. And the Shia militias are pretty much Iranian-sponsored, correct?

General DEMPSEY. I would describe them as Iranian trained and somewhat Iranian equipped.

Senator JOHNSON. Secretary Carter, I think you said that the outcome of Tikrit will explain an awful lot of things. What did you mean by that?

Secretary CARTER. I believe it was General Dempsey who made that statement, so I will let him explain it himself, but I agree with it.

General DEMPSEY. What did I mean by that? [Laughter]

Here is what I meant by that, Senator. There is no doubt that the combination of the popular mobilization forces and the Iraqi Security Forces, they are going to run ISIL out of Tikrit. The question is what comes after in terms of their willingness to let Sunni families move back into their neighborhoods, whether they work to restore the basic services that are going to be necessary, or whether it results in atrocities and retribution. That is what I meant.

Senator JOHNSON. Well, Senator Rubio's line of questioning was laying out our concern that if it is Iran that is at the tip of the spear here, if they are the one sponsoring the victories, they are going to have influence in Iraq, then that is going to be very difficult, very tenuous, very dangerous for the regional peace, correct? Secretary Kerry, do you want to address that one? Are you not concerned about Iran's growing influence in Iraq?

Secretary KERRY. I am concerned about Iran's growing efforts in the region, and we have made it very clear that it is an administration concern, their influence in Yemen, their influence in Beirut and Lebanon, their influence in Syria, in Damascus, and Hezbollah, and of course their influence in Iraq. But I think you have to look historic—I mean, a lot of things are happening in the region, to be honest with you. And the history between Persian Shia and the Arab world and Arab Shia is complicated.

Remember, Iraq and Iran had a 10-year—8 to 10-year war. People were gassed. Iranians did not respond with gas. There were a lot of sort of interesting facets of how that played out. And, yes, Iran's influence has spread at this moment, and we are deeply concerned about it. But if you are concerned about it now, think of what happens, and I hear this—we heard on the floor of the House recently, and you hear it elsewhere—if they had a nuclear weapon and they were doing that.

That is why this administration believes the first step is to prevent the access to the nuclear weapon or prevent their ability to develop a nuclear weapon, and that is our goal, first to try to do that diplomatically. And if it cannot be achieved diplomatically, then we all have a lot of options available to us, but we are eyes wide open with respect to what is happening.

And all of those issues, we have made it clear to our friends in the region, and elsewhere in the world, they do not disappear. If we were to get an agreement to stop them from getting a nuclear weapon—and we are all satisfied that that, in fact, will be the conclusion—we still have all these other issues with Iran, and we all need to be working on the ways in which, and this is exactly what we are doing. GCC members, in fact, will be coming here to Washington in the next month to continue the dialogue we had in the region last week. And I am confident that we will, all of us together, take the steps necessary to counter what Iran is doing in other ways.

Senator JOHNSON. My final point quickly is I am not seeing the full commitment out of this administration, and as a result, we are seeing the growing influence and very dangerous influence of Iran. Thank you, Mr. Chairman.

The CHAIRMAN. Senator Kaine.

Senator KAINE. Thank you, Mr. Chairman, and thank you to the witnesses. We are now in the 8th month of a war that began on the 8th of August. There has not been a congressional authorization of the war, except for the Foreign Relations Committee vote in December. No committee has taken it up. There has been no floor debate. And I view that as highly, highly challenging and disturbing in terms of the way the Nation makes the most grave decision we are supposed to make.

I do agree completely this authorization is needed. Count me among many Members of Congress and others who believe that both the 2001 and 2002 authorizations are not sufficient to cover this military action. If, however, we act to authorize it, there is precedent for congressional authorizations after the beginning of military conflicts. There is that precedent. But if we do not act to authorize it, I think from a legal and precedential standpoint, it would be somewhat catastrophic.

I also agree completely with the testimony of the witnesses that the authorization should be strong and it should be bipartisan for those who are fighting this battle, who have been fighting it without Congress weighing in to indicate whether they think it is in the national interest or not. I cannot imagine asking people to risk their lives with us not having done our job, and if we were to pass it in a narrow way or a partisan way that would not send a message that would make people who risking their lives feel very good about the risk that they are taking.

I want to talk about the ground troop provision from a definitional standpoint, from a mission standpoint. The language, "no enduring offensive ground combat operations," is in the proposed authorization, and it is given some tone and coloration by the President's transmittal letter. The President's transmittal letter says, "My administration's draft AUMF would not authorize long-term, large-scale ground combat operations like those our Nation conducted in Iraq and Afghanistan." And you have used that as sort of a limitation, "not like Iraq or Afghanistan."

Let me ask you this. In the first gulf war, 697,000 American troops were deployed overseas for up to 7 months. Would that be an enduring ground combat operation under this definition?

Secretary CARTER. Senator, I think an operation that large, a state-on-state operation is not something that we foresee as the kind of campaign we would mount against ISIL and not foreseen by this AUMF. If I can just say, the fundamental nature of this campaign, and General Dempsey made this clear, is one in which, and Secretary Kerry also, in which we are seeking the lasting defeat of ISIL. To get a lasting defeat of ISIL, we need to have somebody on the ground who sustains the victory after the ISIL forces are defeated. That is why we are relying—that is why our fight is basically an enabling fight.

Senator KAINE. And, Secretary Carter——

Secretary CARTER. And we are trying to develop the ground forces that would do it. It is very different from the Iraq and Iran—the U.S. assault on——

Senator KAINE. I want to ask you about that very point, but I am trying to figure out is there some meaning to this definition that we could apply to say, no, this is not contemplated. That is what I would like to ask General Dempsey and Secretary Kerry. Six hundred and ninety-seven thousand American troops for 7 months, is that an enduring ground combat operation?

General DEMPSEY. That is not contemplated, to use the words you—the way you characterize them, and it would not lead to the defeat of ISIL. And so, I can say with credibility, no.

Senator KAINE. That that would not be allowed under this language.

General DEMPSEY. That is correct.

Senator KAINE. Secretary Kerry.

Secretary KERRY. I agree.

Senator KAINE. It would not be allowed under this language. With respect to the concept that Secretary Carter raised, and I have raised this with some of you before, the Foreign Relations Committee has had two meetings recently with some of our very strong allies in this mission, King Abdullah of Jordan and Sheikh Tamim, the Emir of Qatar. Qatar is the location of the current combined air operations center at al-Waleed Air Force Base.

The King of Jordan said, "this is not your fight, it is our fight," when we were asking about the ground troops. "This is not your fight, it is our fight. ISIL is born and bred in this region. It is a terrorist threat that is born and bred in this region. They are claiming the mantle of a religion that we revere and they are perverting it for a horrible perverted end, so it is not America's fight. We want your help, but we have to be all in in battling this ourselves."

Sheikh Tamim was even a little clearer when he said, "We do not want American ground troops. We do not want American ground troops because it could send the message that this is the United States against ISIL, or this is the West against ISIL, which could be a recruiting bonanza for ISIL. This needs to be our battle, our ground effort, and we appreciate your support on the airstrike side."

So I am looking for metrics in terms of if we all agree with the proposition that this needs to be a region policing itself with the assistance of the United States, and tell me what that means with respect to what ground troops levels could be appropriate or inappropriate. I mean, just as an example, on the airstrike campaign, of the 2,800 airstrikes, the United States has done 80 percent of the airstrikes. The airstrikes is the not in the region with the United States helping a little bit. We have done 80 percent of the airstrikes.

So what I am worried about with respect to the ground troops is less the words, but the concept, and, Secretary Carter, you were getting at it. This has got to be the region's fight against its own terrorism. If they are willing to be all in, then we should help. But if it gets to the point where we have to contemplate a significant number of ground troops, it almost means that it has been lost from the beginning. If the region will not weigh in to battle their own terrorist threat, there is no amount of ground troops we could put in to Iraq or Syria to win the battles there. We can keep Americans safe here, but we cannot create a recruiting bonanza for ISIL.

So talk to me a little bit about—I understand because the President said in his letter how he would like to use ground troops, and I would rather have an authorization that said that. But I see a real danger of a ground troop creep here converting this into not the region policing its own terrorism, but like the airstrike campaign that is 80 percent U.S. It is a U.S. mission, and I would love your thoughts about how we guard against that, both as a mission matter and as a matter of thinking about how to potentially give them some flesh in the definition.

Secretary KERRY. Well, Senator, I think that everything the President has said, I think this authorization itself in its current form guards against that. But the most significant guard against that is what King Abdullah said and I think General Dempsey, and Secretary Carter, and all of our belief that, you know, the enduring transformation that has to take place here is not going to take place if the United States just comes in and we knock out ISIL and that is it, go away. It is not going to happen. We could do that actually. We have that capacity. But we are not asking to do that, nor are they asking us to do that because I think they understand that the implications of that would be actually to aid in the recruitment to create a bigger problem than we face today.

And in answer to the question that was asked earlier, why does—why do these guys like taking us on to some degree, because if it is just us, that is how they grow, and that is what they want, and we are not getting suckered into that. That is why we built the 62-member coalition. That is why we worked so hard to get these five Arab countries engaged in the kinetic activities with us. It is precisely to deny them that narrative.

And so, as we go forward here, we think the best thing that can happen is what is happening now. This is, in fact, you know, indigenous. It is springing up. The Sunni are gaining confidence in Anbar. There are several battles taking place right now, in fact, not just in Tikrit. There are two others, two out of three where, in fact, we are playing a central role in the other two. It has not been as heralded, but it is making a difference, and the Sunni are prosecuting that.

So as long as we continue to work on the integration, the internal inclusivity of Iraq and its government, as long as we continue to help the Iraqis to be able to do this themselves, help the region to feel empowered by it, that is a long-term recipe for the United States not to have as much risk and not to have to put ourselves on the line in the way we have historically. So we think we are on the right track here. And, in fact, the very strategy we are pursuing adheres to the very standards that you most want to have in place in order to protect against the mission creep.

Senator KAINE. Thank you, Mr. Chairman.

The CHAIRMAN. Senator Flake.

Senator FLAKE. Thank you, Mr. Chairman, and thank you for the testimony. This committee had asked, particularly the chairman.

The committee had asked months and months ago for AUMF language to come from the administration. We are glad that it is here. I think that it is overdue. I think it would have been useful to have that language or some kind of language from the administration early on. I know that the administration was uncomfortable with the language that was passed by this committee in December. I think many of us were uncomfortable with the limitations that were there.

But I think at the same time, we all recognize that we may have to endure some degree of ambiguity in the language, and we are seeing it expressed or manifested here when we talk about what would be considered or what would not in exchange for a resolution that can pass with a bipartisan majority. And that is what I want to just explore for a minute, is at what point does it become—since the administration believes that you have the legal authority to move under the AUMF, at what point does it become not useful to have an AUMF that would be passed simply with a partisan vote, for example? Would that not be useful? Is that worse than no AUMF at all? Secretary Kerry?

Secretary KERRY. Well, is that worse than no AUMF now? Absolutely. I mean, look, we are convinced we have the authority. That is not the issue here, and Senator Johnson asked about that earlier. I mean, we have the authority because ISIL was al-Qaeda. What they changed was their name, and then grew worse. But for years, I think it was about 13 years, somewhere in that vicinity, going back to 2011, it called itself Al Qaeda in Iraq. That is who they were, Al Qaeda in Iraq.

And they have an extensive history of conducting attacks against the U.S. coalition going way back during that period of time. They have had a long relationship between al-Qaeda and Osama bin Laden. They viewed themselves, and still do actually, as the legitimate heirs of the Osama bin Laden mantle. They still view that. They just see themselves in a more aggressive term, and that is why they have some disagreement in tactics with al-Qaeda, whom they separated from. But separating does not change where they came from and who they were when we first engaged in the fight with them. And so, you know, there is a legitimacy to the 2001 effort because it began a long time ago against this very group that simply changed its name and some of its tactics. It does not change the threat to the United States.

So we could obviously and we will continue to prosecute that. But, you know, senators themselves have raised this concern that we are operating under this longest AUMF ever. So there is a much greater clarity and a much greater force that comes from a statement from the Congress that this reincarnated entity and this current metastasizing that is taking place is not going to be tolerated specifically. And that is important.

And frankly, to also answer an earlier question, are there some questions from some people about the staying power of the United States, sometimes you hear that. I hear it in the course of diplomacy, and I think it is important to answer that in this context at this time.

Senator FLAKE. I like Secretary Carter's formulation of what this AUMF needs to do. It needs to provide the necessary flexibility to

wage this campaign, and it needs to send a message to our allies
and to our adversaries that we are in this for the long haul, and
we will back up the efforts of our allies. And frankly, we need to
make clear what the roles of those allies will be.

And so, just to end it, I do believe that an AUMF is certainly
needed here if we have a campaign that is going to go on for a long
time and believe it will go on longer than 3 years. But I am not
troubled by the sunset provision, and certainly we can come back
after 3 years and revisit this with a new administration. And I
might wish for more firm language with regard to what an enduring force or whatever else, but I think we need to value also language that can get a good bipartisan majority to send that message. That is important, too, and as we know, in this body, we
never get everything we want.

So I commend the administration for coming forward, for listening to us on this committee as this AUMF was formulated, and for
consulting and listening to others as well. So I hope we can move
forward, and I appreciate the testimony.

The CHAIRMAN. Thank you. Senator Murphy.

Senator MURPHY. Thank you very much, Mr. Chairman. Thank
you to all of our witnesses. Thank you for your extraordinary ges-
tures to come back to this committee over and over again both in
private and in public to work with us on this the most important
question that the Foreign Relations Committee and the Congress
takes up, the question of when to commit U.S. personnel into war.

I remain as frustrated as many of my colleagues with this question over these definitions. I think the problem is in part every different member of the administration we talk to does seem to have
a slightly different interpretation of what these words mean. And
I cannot blame them because, as I think Secretary Carter said,
there is no historical operational definition of these words. But I
think the lack of consistency has hampered our efforts to get on the
same page together.

And if we resort to just an understanding that these words mean
something less than what happened in Iraq and Afghanistan, then
that really is no limitation at all. And I am barely a lawyer. I prac-
ticed for about 4 years, but I do remember the concept of statutes
being void for vagueness. I fear that this would suffer that same
problem if we were not able to get a consistent understanding of
what those terms mean.

I want to ask one point of clarification on a piece of this termi-
nology, and that is back to Secretary Carter. I was pleased at the
language in the draft from the administration defining "associated
forces," including this limitation that it would be restricted to organizations that were actively engaged in fights against the United
States. But I just want to clarify, you said in your testimony that
it would be limited to associated forces that were actively engaged
against the United States, but the language actually says "engaged
in hostilities against the United States or our coalition partners."

So as to this question of whether Boko Haram is covered under
this, it is not really a question as to whether they are actively engaged in hostilities against the United States so long as they are
engaged in hostilities against a coalition partner. Is it not true that
this authorization would give the United States the ability, subject

to the other restrictions in the authorization, to engage in hostilities against that organization?

Secretary CARTER. I think you are reading it right.

Senator MURPHY. And so, given that reading, let me just ask Senator Menendez's question again. Would Boko Haram, pledging allegiance to ISIS, be covered if the country in which they were engaging in hostilities was a coalition partner of the United States?

Secretary CARTER. Well, I cannot give you a legal answer, but I can give you a common sense answer to that. This is an AUMF that really focuses on the fight against ISIL. We have other authorities, which have already been alluded to in the 2001, which also cover other situations, including some that may involve Boko Haram, that allow us to take action to protect ourselves in that case. But this is really focused on ISIL and the associated forces there when they engage in operations against us or our coalition partners as the text says. And that can be interpreted, but has not yet been interpreted, to cover other groups like Boko Haram.

But just to be clear, under the 2001 authority, and this is important to me because, you know, we have really got to protect ourselves. There are authorities under the 2001 also that could extend to Boko Haram depending upon their behavior and the kind of actions that we needed to take to protect ourselves. So these are always in my experience, and, again, I am not a lawyer. I am just observing this as Secretary of Defense. Our counsels try to interpret the law in such a way that we are acting lawfully and consistent with the intent of the enabling legislation, and that we are able to take actions to protect ourselves. And they do not always—sometimes they get to those determinations when a particular instance arises.

But I think it is important when we have this, and this is the last point I will make, to err on the side of flexibility. I think someone said earlier, well, this language could seem to allow an awful lot, the how part of the provision, and it does. The President—I think if you are hearing different things, the thing I would listen to is what the President said, and he said that this—he does not foresee, and this language does not authorize, the kind of thing that Iraq and Afghanistan represented. And then he gave some examples of the kind of campaign that we intend to wage, which Secretary Kerry noted earlier, ones in which we are enabling a force which provides the lasting victory against ISIL. That is our approach because that is the right approach to getting a lasting victory against ISIL.

But I think in my role and in the chairman's role, some latitude there in the language is appreciated because we need to be able to do what we need to do to protect ourselves. And this encompasses the campaign against ISIL as we now foresee it and I think one can reasonably foresee it, and that is essential because we need to in this campaign.

Senator MURPHY. I have just got a minute remaining. There has been a lot of talk about sending consistent bipartisan messages to our enemies, and I agree. I do not think there has been much division on the message that we have been sending to ISIS. Whether or not we have an authorization, we stand united in our belief that we should take the fight to them.

In the last few days there has been significant division between our two parties on the message that we are sending to Iran, an exceptional, I would argue, unprecedented letter from 47 of our colleagues to the Ayatollah himself that many of us believe will have the effect and has the intention of undermining the authority of the President. Secretary Kerry, you are here before us. This is a subject of great debate within the Senate today. What do you believe are the ramifications of this letter? What do you believe is your interpretation of the facts of that letter, which state essentially that any agreement signed by the United States expires the minute a new President is sworn into office? Share with us your thoughts on whether this is helpful or hurtful to our efforts to try to divorce Iran from any future nuclear ambition.

Secretary KERRY. Well, Senator and members of the committee, my reaction to the letter was utter disbelief. During my 29 years here in the Senate, I never heard of nor even heard of it being proposed anything comparable to this. If I had, I could guarantee you that no matter what the issue and no matter who was President, I would have certainly rejected it.

No one is questioning anybody's right to dissent. Any Senator can go to the floor any day and raise any of the questions that were raised in that. But to write to the leaders in the middle of a negotiation, particularly the leader that they have criticized other people for even engaging with or writing to, to write them and suggest that they are going to give a constitutional lesson, which, by the way was absolutely incorrect, is quite stunning.

This letter ignores more than two centuries of precedent in the conduct of American foreign policy. Formal treaties obviously require the advice of the United States Senate. That is in the Constitution. But the vast majority of international arrangements and agreements do not. And around the world today we have all kinds of executive agreements that we deal with: protection of our troops, the recent agreement we just did with Afghanistan, any number of noncontroversial and broadly supported foreign policy goals. The Executive agreement is a necessary tool of American foreign policy. It has been used by Presidents of both parties for centuries literally, and it is recognized and accepted by Congress from the earliest period of American history.

Now, with respect to the talks, we have been clear from the beginning. We are not negotiating a "legally binding" plan. We are negotiating a plan that will have in it a capacity for enforcement. We do not even have diplomatic relations with Iran right now, and the Senators' letter erroneously asserts that this is a legally binding plan. It is not. That is number one. Number two, it is incorrect when it says that Congress could actually modify the terms of an agreement at any time. That is flat wrong. They do not have the right to modify an agreement reached executive to executive between leaders of the countries.

Now, sure, could another president come in with a different attitude? No President, I think, if this agreement meets its task and does what it is supposed to do in conjunction with China, Russia, France, Germany, Great Britain, all of whom are going to either sign off or not sign off on an agreement. I would like to see the next President, if all of those countries have said this is good and it is working, turn around and just nullify it on behalf of the United States. That is not going to happen.

So I have to tell you that, you know, knowing what we know about this, this risks undermining the confidence that foreign governments in thousands of important agreements commit to between the United States and other countries. And it purports to tell the world that if you want to have any confidence in your dealings with America, they have to negotiate with 535 Members of Congress, and that is both untrue and a profoundly bad suggestion to make, I think.

But aside from the legalities, this letter also raises questions of judgment and policy. We know that there are people in Iran who are opposed to any negotiated arrangement with the P5+1. And we know that a comprehensive solution is not going to happen if Iran's leaders are not willing to make hard choices about the size, and scope, and transparency of their nuclear program. And we know that a nuclear armed Iran is unacceptable.

The CHAIRMAN. Mr. Secretary, I know this is a well written speech, but you have been at this for 5 minutes.

Secretary KERRY. It is not a speech, my friend. This is not a speech. This is a statement about the impact of this irresponsible letter.

The CHAIRMAN. And you have a lot of forums——

Secretary KERRY. And the letter does not have legal authority, and, you know, I think you have to ask what people are trying to accomplish. The author of the letter says he does not want these agreements to be made, and he thinks before the judgment is even made that it is a mistake. So we will see where we wind up.

The CHAIRMAN. Thank you.

Secretary KERRY. But I am asked by one Senator the impact, and I am laying out to the committee what the impact is. And I am sorry if people up here do not want to hear it.

The CHAIRMAN. And 5 minutes and 26 seconds later you finished. I will say that I did not sign the letter. I am very disappointed, though, that you have gone back on your statement that any agreement must pass muster with Congress. The way we pass muster here is we vote, and I think all of us are very disappointed with the veto threat and the stiff-arming that has taken place. But with that——

Secretary KERRY. But, Senator, let me—Mr. Chairman, let me just——

The CHAIRMAN. Senator Gardner.

Secretary KERRY. Mr. Chairman.

Senator GARDNER. Thank you, Mr. Chairman.

Secretary KERRY. You have the right to vote any day you want.

Senator GARDNER. Mr. Chairman, thank you for the time.

Secretary KERRY. You can——

Senator GARDNER. Secretary Carter, Secretary Kerry, General Dempsey, I want to thank you all for testifying today. This issue of an authorization for the use of military force is one of the most serious issues that Congress can consider, and I look forward to our committee's hearings and consideration of the President's draft AUMF.

I am concerned about perhaps mixed messages from the administration regarding the ISIL threat. On March 3, General Austin stated that ISIL is losing its fight against us, yet only a week earlier on February 26, Director of National Intelligence Clapper said the organization remains, "a formidable and brutal threat and is increasing its influence outside of Iraq and Syria."

The threat from ISIL is real and requires a carefully coordinated strategy to ensure their complete destruction. I look forward to hearing from you today on defining the breadth and scope of our mission and how we can work together in ensuring its bipartisan success. I remain open-minded as to what gets the most support, but I want to understand the details and to fully know that we are not unnecessarily restraining or restricting our ability to win.

To Secretary Carter, in your remarks you state that, again, I quote from your statement—your remarks, excuse me. "I cannot tell you our campaign to defeat ISIL will be completed in 3 years," that you believe that the sunset clause proposed by the President is a sensible and principled provision. You have heard Senator Johnson, Senator Flake, Senator Cardin, Secretary Kerry all talk about this. If the AUMF is not authorized within 3 years, the next President could continue using other legal authority, such as the 2001 AUMF. Is that correct?

Secretary CARTER. That is correct. That is the legal interpretation of the AUMF, although I should note that the intent—stated intent—of the President is to revisit the 2001 AUMF after this one as well. He has said that, and that is a totally different subject. But I would just note it.

Senator GARDNER. In your verbal comments here, you stated that what a shame it would be to have a safe haven for ISIL. And I believe you were referring to the geographic limitation. Could the 3-year time limitation, though, be interpreted as a safe haven as well?

Secretary CARTER. It certainly should not be. It is not by anyone involved in drafting the AUMF. As I said, it is not a number or time period derived from our thinking about the campaign. It is derived from our Constitution and from the election cycle, and it is for sure in our system that there will be a new President in 3 years. It is for sure that he or she will have had 1 year, as Secretary Kerry said, to get themselves on their feet, and, therefore, it foresees—it leaves latitude for this to be revisited.

That is something I respect as a consequence of our political system. It is not a consequence of the battlefield dynamics or the campaign we are waging. Obviously we hope to wrap it up as soon as possible, but I specifically said, and I believe I cannot tell you it will be over in 3 years.

Senator GARDNER. And I think we have had testimony from others who have talked about the ability to go for 3 years, that we would not be able to actually defeat in 3 years, but what we would be able to do in 3 years. And so, is 3 years the right time? If you are going to put a time limit, should it be 4? Should it be no time limit?

Secretary CARTER. Again, the number three has to do with our political system, not with the defeat of ISIS. Now, you can argue—I respect people who want to not have a sunset or something, but

I do not think—I think the logic of 3 years derives from the nature of our political system. There is no foreseeing, in my judgment, how long it will take to defeat ISIL any more than you can begin any kind of military campaign and be sure exactly how long it will take.

Senator GARDNER. Thank you. And, Secretary Carter, you said in your comments, too, that "enduring," and I believe it was in response to Senator Cardin, that "enduring" is not Iraq and Afghanistan. Can you give any more of a clear definition than that, the term "enduring?"

Secretary CARTER. The President when he explained the provision which describes how the campaign is authorized to be waged, explained that there—he was not telling—he was not saying, and this is very sensible to me, enumerating the things that we could do. He was setting a limit, which is the language of "enduring offensive ground combat operations," to mean something like Iraq and Afghanistan, not foreseen in our campaign, not asking for authority for it. He also gave some illustrations of what it meant.

Senator GARDNER. Just to follow—just to go back on that, and I am sorry to interrupt. So, I mean, that is the definition of the best we can get, though, is not Iraq or Afghanistan on the term "enduring."

Secretary CARTER. Well, it is an important principle, I think, that the AUMF reflects that makes sense to me not to try to enumerate everything that we may find it necessary to do in the course of this campaign. Instead, the text sets an outer limit. It does not try to enumerate everything. The President's language did illustrate some things, and Secretary Kerry cited them, but it does not try to say everything that we might have to do. And that is a good, sensible thing for a military campaign. You cannot know everything you are going to do.

Senator GARDNER. Thank you, Secretary Carter. I have two more questions I want to follow up. Secretary Kerry, in response to Senator Rubio, you had said that, I believe, that several of the Middle East counterparts that you have been talking to, you have shared with them details or some details of the negotiations with Iran. Am I misunderstanding your response?

Secretary KERRY. We have shared with them an outline of it. We have not shared with them—actually we have briefed them. We had our team go down and brief them and give them——

Senator GARDNER. On the details of at least——

Secretary KERRY. Well, some of the details, yes.

Senator GARDNER. Are those the same details that we have been briefed on?

Secretary KERRY. You have gotten a much greater in-depth——

Senator GARDNER. Okay. I was just making sure. Thank you. And to—I believe to General Dempsey, talking about the peshmerga a little bit, in terms of percentage, if you look at the ISF overall, if you look at some of the fighting that is taking place and the efforts to undertake it against ISIL, what weight of effort would you say that the peshmerga or other fighting in the region are we currently pursuing against ISIL?

General DEMPSEY. The early successes against ISIL were largely through the peshmerga, and that will evolve over time. But they have been carrying the majority of the effort thus far.

Senator GARDNER. And by "majority of effort," is there a way—are they carrying out a third, three-quarters, 90 percent, the weight of effort?

General DEMPSEY. No, Senator, I cannot actually put a percentage on it. But the early effort to blunt ISIL's momentum were in the north, and, therefore, with the peshmerga.

Senator GARDNER. And reports in the news and other places have stated that the peshmerga are only getting about 10 percent of the arms that have been routed through Baghdad. Is that correct?

General DEMPSEY. Again, I do not have the percentage. I can certainly take it for the record. But there was some friction early on with the willingness of the Government of Iraq to provide weapons to the peshmerga, but we think we have managed our way through that.

[The written response to the question above follows:]

The peshmerga are receiving a higher percentage of arms and ammunition delivered to Iraq then the reported 10 percent. As of 14 April 2015, the Ministry of Peshmerga has received approximately 41 percent of the munitions and 61 percent of the weapon's systems delivered to Iraq. These numbers include all USG programs (Foreign Military Financing, Foreign Military Sales, Iraq Train and Equip Fund, Excess Defense Articles, Presidential Drawdown Authority) as well as coalition donations.

Senator GARDNER. And so, right now you feel confident that the problem we faced in seeing that arms reach Erbil has now been settled and resolved?

General DEMPSEY. I am confident that we broke through the initial friction, but it does not mean it will not recur.

Senator GARDNER. Thank you. Thank you, Mr. Chairman.

The CHAIRMAN. Senator Shaheen.

Senator SHAHEEN. Thank you, Mr. Chairman, and thank you, Secretary Kerry, and Secretary Carter, and General Dempsey, for being here.

I was very pleased when the administration sent over language for the AUMF. I supported the AUMF that passed out of this committee in the last Congress because I think, as you all have said, that it is very important for our men and women who may be putting themselves at the risk in the fight against ISIL to know that they have the support of Congress. I think it is very important for the American public to know—to hear this debate and to have—to know that Congress is supporting whatever action that we take.

And with respect to that, one of the places where I think I would have issue with the language that was sent over by the administration is with respect to the reporting on the ongoing actions. As you all know, the language in the AUMF that the administration sent over says that the President shall report to Congress at least once every 6 months on specific actions taken pursuant to this authorization.

In looking at the AUMF that passed the committee in December, the reporting requirements are much more robust and much more comprehensive. So it requests reporting every 60 days. It also requests a comprehensive strategy report that would be clear to Congress and, therefore, to the American people, the specific political and diplomatic objectives of the United States in the region. It asks for clearly defined military objectives, and the list goes on.

And while I appreciate that there may be concern on the part of the executive branch and the military about the level of detail that is requested in that AUMF, it still seems to me that there is a benefit from providing additional detail about the mission and more frequent periodic reporting. I think that is important not just for Congress. I think there are also some benefits to the operation because it makes it very clear in writing at some level what the plan is. And, you know, I was always taught that a plan is not a plan unless you have written it down somewhere, unless you have got something that you can refer to.

So can I ask you first, I think, Secretary Kerry, if you would respond to that, and then perhaps Secretary Carter and General Dempsey might want to as well.

Secretary KERRY. Senator, of course—I mean, first of all, believe me, the plan is reduced to writing, and the President reviews it, and there are an enormous amount of analysis that goes into this. So you are right certainly that, you know, it needs to be specific. But I think there is a balance between the amount of time and the numbers of efforts that are put into reporting versus fighting the war, getting the job done.

Senator SHAHEEN. Sure.

Secretary KERRY. And I think you do not want to tie people—I mean, I have asked the State Department to do a review of all the reports that we have to do, and the numbers of people, and the person hours that are put into reports that frankly do not often do not get thoroughly read or digested.

And so, I think there is a briefing process that my memory here works pretty well, and 6 months, when you think of it, is a pretty fair amount of time. It is not so much time in the course of this in terms of the review that it does not do the job when you mix it also with the numbers of classified briefings, hearings that will take place, and so forth.

So, look, we are not trying to resist accountability, I assure you. But surely we could find a way to balance so that there is not, you know, an excess of paper turning and process that actually gets in the way of getting things done. I think there is a balance personally. I have not talked to my colleagues about it, but I would assume, I think, they might feel the same way.

Senator SHAHEEN. And certainly I would agree that there is a balance. I am just questioning whether the balance in the language that has been sent over is the right balance. I do not know, Secretary Carter, if you or General Dempsey want to add anything.

Secretary CARTER. I think "balance" is the right word, and you are both seeking that. And I agree with the principle.

General DEMPSEY. And I would just add, Senator, it is for you to determine how to exercise your oversight authority. But it was aligned somewhat with the way we do our war powers reporting, and that may—there was a logic to that.

Senator SHAHEEN. Thank you. I want to make sure I understood something that I think you said, Secretary Carter, and that was that—I did not get this quote down exactly correct—But you said something about believing that the 2001 AUMF gives us the ability to protect ourselves if we are attacked. Did I understand that accurately?

Secretary CARTER. Well, it is more specific than that, and, of course, the legal interpretation is more specific than that. But I was simply saying that the existence of that since 2001 has provided the authority under which we have protected ourselves, and it is quite clear that we have needed to protect ourselves. And it is as simple as that.

Senator SHAHEEN. But the question I have is did we need that AUMF to protect ourselves if attacked. What I am trying to figure out is why—is whether we should put—insert specific language in this AUMF that acknowledges that the fight that we are engaged in now is one that is covered by this AUMF, and, therefore, the 2001 is not part of the action that we are doing now.

Secretary CARTER. I will explain my understanding, and then ask Secretary Kerry to add. The text of the AUMF that has been submitted explicitly states that this supersedes the 2002 AUMF. And the President has also indicated his willingness——

Senator SHAHEEN. Right. That I understand.

Secretary CARTER [continuing]. His willingness and, I think, his desire to revisit the 2001 AUMF. The only thing I would say is that it is important that as we do that, I understand the desire to revisit the 2001 AUMF. We do need the continuing authority that this new one does not provide to continue to protect us against others, not ISIL. We need some authority to do that in order to protect the country. And if we replace the 2001, that is fine with me as long as it gives us the authority to protect ourselves.

Senator SHAHEEN. Can we just get a clarification, Mr. Chairman? I have seen press reports that the White House is open to Congress inserting language—legislative language on this point as we did when we passed out of the committee the AUMF in December. Secretary Kerry, do you have—do you know if that is correct, if the administration would accept that kind of language?

Secretary KERRY. I do not specifically know if the decision had been made to accept language, though I do know specifically that the President has said that, and it would sort of invite the notion of language because he has said that if you pass an AUMF with respect to ISIL now, he will rely on his authority for ISIL on that AUMF and not the 2001, so that would seem to leave it open. I just do not want to conclusively say they would accept language because I have not personally heard that signed off.

Senator SHAHEEN. Thank you. Thank you, Mr. Chairman.

The CHAIRMAN. Senator Perdue.

Senator PERDUE. Thank you, Mr. Chairman. I have a question for Chairman Dempsey. But first, I just want to thank you personally for your lifetime of service, and I hope that you will take my echo of the request earlier to give our condolences to these heroes that lost their lives last night.

In his recent address before Congress, the Israeli Prime Minister Netanyahu stated, "So when it comes to Iran and ISIL, the enemy of your enemy is your enemy." Would you respond to that from a military perspective for me?

General DEMPSEY. Well, I will not respond to the Prime Minister's choice of words or how he determines his national interests. But in terms of our national interests, as I mentioned, we have six things that concern us about Iran. One of them happens to be their nuclear program.

Senator PERDUE. Thank you. A followup on that is after two wars and 14 years later, as Secretary Carter reminded us earlier this morning, al-Qaeda still exists. That is not a criticism. It is just a reality. I would like for you to help me define what we seek from a military point of view, what a victory is with ISIL in this—with regard to this AUMF and our current task ahead of us.

General DEMPSEY. Yes, thanks for asking, Senator. We actually rarely have the chance to talk about the overall scheme here, if you will. So ISIL is transregional, which is to say they are not just confined to Iraq and Syria. They are generational, which is to suggest the duration of this campaign will be prolonged. We are seeking to find a sustainable level of effort.

And when I say that, you know, I did not have the chance to respond to the difference in AUMFs from 1941 to 2015. It is important to note that the use of military force in a state-on-state conflict is very different than the use of military force in a state on a nonstate actor. And so, the military brings three things, and we own two lines of effort out of nine against ISIL. The other lines of effort are governance, countermessaging, counter foreign financing, humanitarian relief, and so forth.

The two things that we are doing is, of course, using direct action, and notably with our airstrikes. And the other is building partner capacity, which is to say building up the ability of the Peshmerga, the Iraqi security forces, and the Sunni tribal leaders to reject ISIL because it will only be permanently defeated if they reject the ideology, not simply by us cutting off its head. It has actually got to be rejected from within, and that requires a different application of the military instrument than it would be if we were fighting a state-on-state actor.

One last thing, and then in the interest of time I will stop. The military does three things for this Nation: direct action, build partners, and enable others. The best example we have right now of enabling others is what we are doing with the French in Mali against al-Qaeda of the Islamic Maghreb. So that is what we are doing. That is what this AUMF allows. And the limiting principle, I sense we are looking, or some of us in the room are looking, for a limiting principle. The limiting principle is the way this particular enemy will be defeated. It will not be defeated by U.S. military power alone.

Senator PERDUE. Thank you. You mentioned last week, Mr. Chairman, that you were concerned about what happens with regards to sectarian violence and so forth. And if we are victorious against ISIL in Iraq, it looks to me like that Iran is also victorious because of their efforts there behind the Shia militia. Can you speak to that just a minute in terms of that part of the definition of victory? And then what do we do from a military standpoint once we declare victory over ISIL in Iraq and Syria, by the way?

General DEMPSEY. There is a lot in that question.

Senator PERDUE. Yes, sir.

General DEMPSEY. Look, Iran is going to be influential in Iraq, has been influential in Iraq, and I am concerned about the way they wield that influence. There are ways they could wield it to promote a better Iraq economically, for example, and there are ways they can wield that influence to create a state where the Sunni and the Kurds are no longer welcome. And it is my concern about the latter that we are watching carefully as this Tikrit event unfolds.

As far as declaring victory against ISIL, that is not for us to declare. As I said, very much we can enable it. We can support a coalition, hold the coalition together. We can build into the region. We can harden the region against it militarily. But the ideology has to be defeated by those in the region.

Senator PERDUE. Well, I am concerned about Iran's stature in the region, particularly relative to Assad and Hezbollah as well as the Shia militia. And so, this looks like that if we are successful, we have a partner in crime here where Iran is also going to be successful and strengthen their position.

Let me echo one thing that I heard both sides say this morning, and I want you to pass this along to your men and women in service, if you will, is that we hope we will end up unified. I absolutely believe we have to be like-minded in this. This is bigger than any partisan position. This is about the security of our country. And the lesson we heard from the speech from last week was simply this, and that is this is bigger than the Middle East. It is bigger than our national security. This is about global security all of a sudden.

I would like to follow up real quick if I could on this symmetric versus asymmetric conversation, though. You are talking about the symmetric or the asymmetric question with regard to Iraq, Syria, and the Middle East right now. I am a concerned a little bit, and I would like to have you respond, if you will, and maybe Secretary Carter as well. What impact does this have on our long-term strategy relative to the symmetric threats? And I know that we do not talk a lot about the People's Republic of China. We do not talk about Russia in this conversation. But it is all interrelated, and I would like to see how this in your mind relates to the longer term strategy.

General DEMPSEY. Thanks, Senator. So for the first time in my 40 years, we have both state and nonstate threats to our national interests because in my first 25 years it was all about state threats, notably the Soviet Union. For the last 15 years, it is all about nonstate actors. We live now in an environment where we have threats emanating from both states and nonstates, and it makes— we are actually adapting quite well to that. And I do not want to turn this into a budget hearing, but if we do not get some budget help on this issue of sequestration, it is going to be very difficult to manage both threats.

Senator PERDUE. Thank you, sir. Thank you, Mr. Chairman.

The CHAIRMAN. Thank you, Senator. For you not to get a word in about your budget would be a remissful thing on your part.

Senator Markey.

Senator MARKEY. Thank you, Mr. Chairman. And I want to thank Secretary Kerry for his strong words about the letter that was sent by our 47 colleagues to the Government of Iran. I think that was a serious breach of protocol and exercise in bad judgment, especially at this very sensitive time. And I thank the Secretary for taking that very strong position in this hearing.

Secretary Carter, what I would like to ask you is how this extends to Libya, and what this authorization could mean given the increasing stronghold that ISIS has in many parts of Libya, and what it could portend in terms of U.S. commitment to the removal of ISIL from Libya.

Secretary CARTER. Senator, thank you. There are those in Libya who are, I will use the term, rebranding themselves as ISIL. That is not the only place we see that, but it is certainly going on in Libya. And, therefore, this AUMF could apply to operations in and around Libya against those groups, depending upon their behavior and whether they have met this criteria of this AUMF. And also because the 2001 AUMF is extant as well, that could also cover actions we might need to take in Libya as it has in the past if there are successor groups to al-Qaeda. So both of those might apply to Libya, and these are the kinds of things, determinations that are made as these cases arise.

But you do see in this social media fueled movement called ISIL people who are wannabes or want to join or have been associated with al-Qaeda or some other group who are putting up the flag of ISIL. And we need to recognize that that is a characteristic of the campaign, and that is why the AUMF has the language that it does.

Senator MARKEY. And if I may move back over to Syria in terms of what all of this means for a long-term American commitment, our goal is to remove Assad. The goal of Iran and Russia is to keep Assad in office, Iran most prominently given their now Crescent move from Baghdad over through Tehran into Damascus.

What does this mean in terms of the commitment that we are making to have the moderate Syrians depose, take out, Assad? That is their goal. Are we committing to back them in their effort to depose Assad because that is their stated public goal. So how do we square up this AUMF potentially with that longer term goal, which our principal allies inside of Syria would have?

Secretary KERRY. Senator, this is ISIL specific. There are those who wish it would include Assad, but it does not. We are supporting the moderate opposition, however, very directly in the efforts that are focused on Assad. And the Congress, and we are grateful for it, has approved the training and equip program. Some $500 million have been appropriated. And that program is about to be up and running. In addition to that, there are other activities, as you know, that are focused on the issue of President Assad. But specific to the AUMF, the AUMF is ISIL specific, and it does not authorize activities against Assad.

Senator MARKEY. But in helping to fight ISIL inside of Syria and strengthening the moderate Syrians, whose goal is to remove Assad, are we not at a minimum indirectly helping that goal to be achieved by potentially eliminating the threat of ISIL to that goal of the moderate Syrians? And are we contemplating as a result then a longer stay in Syria to accomplish that goal as well?

Secretary KERRY. No, I think when you say "a stay in Syria," we are not in Syria.

Senator MARKEY. No, I mean, stay in terms of our military support for——

Secretary KERRY. The military support is——

Senator MARKEY [continuing]. Taking out ISIL and strengthening the moderate Syrians.

Secretary KERRY. We are committed to strengthening the moderate Syrians. We are committed to help train and equip. We are committed to other activities that are specifically focused on the Assad regime. But this authorization and the efforts to deal with ISIL are focused on degrading and destroying ISIL. And that particular military activity, should that goal be accomplished, would then cease and desist. But the effort to support the moderate opposition will continue.

Now, obviously if ISIL is eliminated and the moderate opposition has gained capacity as a consequence of that particular fight, they are going to be strengthened in their other activities. And we have made that argument openly and publicly.

Senator MARKEY. How long, in your opinion, General, do you think it will take for Assad to be removed militarily or politically given his current state?

General DEMPSEY. Well, it is two very different questions. I mean, the diplomatic line of effort is the primary line of effort right now. I have not been asked to apply military—the military line of effort to the removal of Assad, so I think I would actually defer to others on how long it might take. I mean, the position of the United States was clear, and that is that he has given up the legitimacy of governing people who he is oppressing.

Senator MARKEY. Thank you.

The CHAIRMAN. If I could, and just to respond to Senator Markey and Secretary Kerry's previous comment, I would like to ask unanimous consent to enter into the record a copy of Congress.gov where then-Senator Kerry and then-Senator Obama cosponsored a bill to ensure that Congress had a vote on the agreement that we reach with Iraq. I understand that in this world sometimes where you stand is where you sit, but I would like to balance out some of the discussion today and understand that certainly positions change sometimes depending on which side of the table you are sitting.

[The information referred to was not available when this transcript went to press.]

The CHAIRMAN. And with that, Senator Isakson.

Senator MARKEY. If I may, Mr. Chairman, I was referring to the timing of the delivery of that letter given the negotiations which Secretary Kerry is right now engaged in. And, again, I continue to believe that was an inappropriate document for the time at which it was delivered, just not timely.

The CHAIRMAN. Thank you.

Senator ISAKSON. Thank you, Mr. Chairman. Thank you all for your service to the country. We appreciate your patience here today. I had a college professor who once said the mind can only absorb what seat can endure. You have been enduring a lot of time, and we hope we will not keep you much longer.

I have one question, and it is for Secretary Kerry, and it is not a deference to you that I am asking the question. I want to thank you for your service. You do a great job for the American people, and you work—you have a job that has a Commander in Chief who is a politician, who is subject to 535 other politicians and your funding. So any question I ask you would not be really fair if it had a political connotation to it.

But, Secretary Kerry, you and I have served together a long time. You served the country in Vietnam. You have been a great leader for our country. And you know this is really a political issue in part, and has political overturns in terms of the AUMF, which I do support. And I believe that Senator—the remarks made by Senator Menendez, Senator Flake, Senator Perdue, and others about the need to come together as a Congress and have a meaningful AUMF are important.

Here is what I want to ask you, Secretary Kerry. The first President to ever mention radical Islam was Thomas Jefferson and the Barbary pirates. General Dempsey has talked about this being an enduring conflict, and talked about it being regionally—evolving regionally and being transregional. We know that ISIL is in the Maghreb through Boko Haram. They are in the Levant. We have had attacks in Paris. We have had attacks in Brussels. So it is a growing threat.

Here is my question. If, in fact, we have had problems all the way dating back to Thomas Jefferson, and, in fact, this is a growing regional threat, having a time limitation on the AUMF does not make a lot of sense to me because I think we have a united commitment as a country and as a Nation to fight ISIL and to defeat ISIL. But as General Dempsey has said, that definition is not the easiest definition to write into words. It is a combination of a lot of things happening together, one of which is an enduring commitment.

On the term of "enduring," I think enduring in terms of the AUMF means it does not mean special forces, but it probably would mean 672,000 troops being deployed. And I can understand that is something the President would probably want to come back to the Congress and get an authorization for. But if we took off the 3-year limitation so that this was a commitment until we accomplish our goal of degrading and destroying ISIL, would we not be better off to send the clear signal that there is no end to this conflict as we are concerned until we win the victory? And that was probably a disjointed question and more of a statement, but I would appreciate your response.

Secretary KERRY. Thank you, Senator. No, it is a very important one actually, and I appreciate it.

Senator ISAKSON. And you do not have to commit yourself on behalf of the administration, but thought-provoking comments, I would like to hear them.

Secretary KERRY. Well, thank you. First of all, let me thank you personally because I am delighted you stayed on the committee. I see you gave up a couple of seats of seniority to do so, and I well know why you did. And I certainly want to express my appreciation because I know you will be a strong and critical voice for some of the things that do not always get paid attention to, particularly in Africa. So I thank you for that.

I do not think there is any doubt—I mean, I believe that the 3 years, if they are accompanied by the vote that is necessary here, and by the accompanying commitments by each senator who goes to the floor and speak and define why we are doing this and what we are doing, I think would be a healthy debate. I am confident coming out of that will be an absolute understanding by everybody in the region and in the world that we are deeply committed to this and committed for more than the 3 years.

I think the 3 years will be respected, as Secretary Carter said, as a reflection of the kind of political process here, and not as a diminishment of the fundamental commitment to achieve our goal. Every country in the region is committed to defeat ISIL, every country. And that is particularly what has prompted some of the questions here because of Iran's commitment to do that.

So I really think that the 3 years is more of a statement of respect by President Obama of personal choice for him to say to the next President and to the Congress, review this, take a look at it, see how it is going, tweak it if necessary. I do not think he has any doubt about the readiness and willingness of Congress to continue that forward, but perhaps with some, you know, state-of-the-art refinements.

So I do not think it is a problem. I think we can deal with that, and I think in order to achieve the vote that is necessary, the experience of Iraq and the experience of Afghanistan, you know, create a sufficient cloud over the potential of this vote that I think everybody can say, okay, what is the matter with doing—you know, reviewing it in three years, but let us go do it. And I think that is the commitment that we need, and that gets us the stronger vote to do that.

Senator ISAKSON. Well, I appreciate your response. I would just ask you to take that message back and massage it a little bit and think about what I said, because I think the unequivocal commitment to see it to the end is important to be sent. And I think the enduring presence gives you a chance to come back and revisit it if we expand our military operations. But in the meantime that we have a common ground to get the vote out necessary to send a clear signal that Congress and the White House are united. Thank you for your time and your service.

Secretary KERRY. Thank you, Senator.

The CHAIRMAN. Senator Coons.

Senator COONS. Thank you, Chairman Corker. I want to start by thanking General Dempsey and Secretary Carter and Secretary Kerry for your service, for your testimony, your engagement with us today. We recently heard of tragic news of 11 service members, four soldiers, seven marines currently missing and, I believe, presumed lost in a training accident at Elgin Air Force Base. And I just think it is worth a moment of prayerful reflection on the enormous sacrifice that they have and that their families—the loss that they are facing. Dover Air Force Base will be the place to which those families now go and their remains returned. And I think all of us who are contemplating the undertaking we are about to authorize, that I pray we are about to authorize, is one that will involve a great deal of sacrifice across many countries and many years.

A question I wanted to raise is about who bears the cost. In addition to the men and women of the Armed Forces and their families,

I think we need to be putting on the table in our conversation about authorizing the conflict against ISIS the financial cost. General Dempsey was right to raise the concerns about DOD's budget for maintenance of effort across many different fields. The need to pay for this war is, for me, a central concern going back to 1961 when President Eisenhower said America could choke itself to death piling up military expenditures just as surely as it can defeat itself by not paying enough for protection.

We have used a combination of either spending cuts or increased revenue to pay for every conflict before the 2003 Iraq war, and the two post-9/11 engagements added literally trillions of dollars toward the Nation's debt.

So I think we cannot write another blank check for a war. We have to pay for it. I think it is not only fiscally responsible, but morally responsible, and engages every American in bearing the cost of the conflict. And I am aware this is not directly within the purview of this committee, but I think it is the responsibility of all of Congress.

So I am intending to renew this conversation. In the last Congress I introduced an amendment to the AUMF that was debated and considered, and I will do so in this debate and consideration, and also in the upcoming budget process. I wondered if any of you cared to comment on behalf of the administration on an amendment that would call for a temporary war surtax that raises revenues, or one that is a mix of raising revenues and cutting spending, to offset the cost of the conflict against ISIL. Secretary Carter, I will start with you, if I might.

Secretary CARTER. You are raising a very important question. My own view is that question is not best associated with the authorization for the use of military force, although it is a very important question. The AUMF principally covers the kind of campaign required and the support and authority of the President to engage in that.

With respect to the expenditures, we are in a situation, and Chairman Dempsey referred to this, and I believe the State Department also in terms of its own budget, of one in which we have had year after year of turmoil, which is disruptive, which is wasteful, which causes all of us, and I think this is probably true in the State Department budget and any of my other colleagues, to have a very difficult time managing appropriately and efficiently. So that is a very important problem.

And I appreciate your attention to it, and agree with what you said. Again now, I am offering a view off the top of the head here, but I think that that is best dealt with and needs to be dealt with, but best dealt with in another way than by incorporating the funding situation in the AUMF. And I will say one more thing. Well, I think that is——

Senator COONS. Thank you, Mr. Secretary. The point I am simply trying to raise is that at the same time that the Chairman of the Joint Chiefs raises appropriately, enduring budget concerns. As a former member of the Budget Committee myself, I feel uncomfortable that we continue to use OKO contingency funding for more and regions, more and more functions. And I would like to see us take on perhaps in other committees the responsibility of clearly shouldering the responsibility of paying for this and not just asking for sacrifice from those who wear the uniform.

Secretary Kerry, if I might, two questions in the time I have left. There has been some back and forth and a number of questions by senators about what "associated forces" mean. Both Senator Isakson and I have long been engaged in issues relating to Africa, as you well know, and whether in Libya or in Nigeria. There have recently been organizations pledging their allegiance to ISIL. Just this past Saturday Boko Haram leader, Abubakar Shekau pledged allegiance in a statement that they posted to their Twitter account. And I think the conflict with Boko Haram and Nigeria is another frankly good example of a situation where an American boots on the ground presence is not what is called for. An American effort to facilitate and support efforts by the Nigerians and their regional allies is the best strategy going forward.

But in your view, if that began to take off and their conflict began to engage some of our coalition partners, would this AUMF qualify for us to go after any groups that have pledged allegiance? And then what are the actions they need to take against coalition partners or Americans in order to be covered by the AUMF in its current language?

Secretary KERRY. Well, Senator, thank you for the question, an important one. As of now at this moment in its current state, merely by pledging as they have pledged, or flying the flag, or, you know, saying that they are now affiliated, there is no decision made nor any contemplated that they would be covered under this at this moment. I mean, that is not adequate. But if, as Secretary Carter said, they start to attack the United States or join with ISIL in a specific strategy to attack coalition partners, that would raise a legitimate question, and this authorization could, in fact, under those circumstances cover them. It would have to be—you know, there would be a lot of internal scrubbing of exactly what those activities were, what the implications are and so forth. It would not be automatic, but it would be open to judgment.

Senator COONS. Let me ask one last question, if I might, Mr. Secretary, on the topic of the negotiations with Iran. I will make a statement, and if you care to comment, that would be great. It is my hope that if a long-term agreement is reached, that the inspection obligations, the IAEA inspection obligations will be enduring and will not simply sunset at the end of whatever that term is. And I think knowing that there was a continuing inspection obligation would give some comfort to those of us who do not trust Iran and are not confident that at the end of the window they will not simply immediately return to their previous illicit nuclear weapons activities. Do you care to make a comment?

Secretary KERRY. I will make a very quick comment, and it addresses a lot of the comments that we have been hearing from the Hill over the course of the last weeks and months. I keep hearing people say we do not trust Iran, we do not trust Iran. Nothing in this agreement contemplated, if it gets reached, is based on trust. Nothing. In fact, it is based on distrust, and, therefore, would have to be accompanied by an adequate level of verification, whatever that may be. I am not going to discuss at all what might or might not be contemplated, but I will just simply say to you whatever agreement is reached is not on the basis of some words in a document and trust. It has to be verified. It has to be accountable.

Senator COONS. Thank you, Mr. Secretary. Thank you, Mr. Chairman.

The CHAIRMAN. Senator Risch.

Senator RISCH. Thank you, Mr. Chairman. General Dempsey, this question is for you. First of all, let me state this as a statement. I appreciate what you are doing here. I think all of us agree that we need a strong vote on this AUMF, and I appreciate your efforts, Senator Kerry—or, excuse me, Secretary Kerry, to put this together. And this is a very difficult needle to thread because of the wide variance of views in Congress. So I appreciate your efforts to do that, and I am hoping at the end of the day that we do have this strong—a strong vote in support of this. So I urge you to continue those efforts.

General Dempsey, this question is for you. If this passes, how will things be different after this passes than they are now? What is this going to change?

General DEMPSEY. I do not think there will be any difference in our activities. I think there will be potentially a difference among our coalition partners in the way they view our commitment to the fight. But in terms of the way we apply military force either directly through partners or enabling others, it will not change.

Senator RISCH. Okay. Thank you very much. Mr. Chairman, this—what I am going to say now is a statement for the record. It is not a question. And I want to respond to some of the comments that were made here today.

I am one of the 47 senators that signed the letter that there has been all this talk about in recent days. You know, this indignation and breast beating over this letter is absolute nonsense. Each of us that signed that is an elected Member of the United States Senate, and as such is a member of the first branch of this government. To say that we should not be communicating is nonsense.

Members of Congress every single day communicate with members of other countries, with Presidents, and heads of other countries, with Secretaries of State and Foreign Ministers from other countries. It is done regularly. Every time Congress has a recess, loads of airplanes leave Andrews Air Force Base with dozens of Members of Congress who go directly and meet face-to-face with these heads of state. This letter was nothing more. We have constitutional responsibilities, that we as elected officials of this first branch of government, are required to meet.

The problem we have got here is we have a real disagreement over the talk regarding this treaty. And let there be no mistake, this is a treaty that is being negotiated. Secretary Kerry and I were on opposite sides when we were debating the New START agreement. That was a treaty, an agreement, between two nations regarding their nuclear capabilities. This is the exact same thing. It is an attempt to reach an agreement over nuclear weapons capability with another nation. It is a treaty and should be treated as such. I hope an agreement is reached. I really hope we get a good agreement. If we do not get a good agreement, there should be no agreement.

I will say in regards to what Secretary Kerry said about other countries in the region and their view of what is happening here, he conceded that they were nervous. I would go further than that. I meet with the same people. I would classify their feeling about this as queasy, very queasy, and anybody who doubts that should get the transcript of what Prime Minister Netanyahu said about it last week. I think the characterization that he made of how he feels, his country feels, is very representative of how other countries in the region feel.

Mr. Chairman, that is a statement for the record. I yield back my time. Thank you.

The CHAIRMAN. Senator Paul.

Senator PAUL. Thank you, Mr. Chairman, and thank you to the panel for coming today. Madison wrote that history demonstrates what the Constitution supposed that the executive branch is most prone to war, and, therefore, the Constitution, with studied care, vested that power in the legislature. Madison also went on to further write that the separation of powers would be protected by pitting the ambitions of one branch against the ambitions of another. There will be points of dispute. These points of dispute are important, and no one side will monolithically be able to declare victory.

But I can tell you I am not particularly happy with being lectured to by the administration about the Constitution. This is an administration who I believe has trampled the Constitution at many turns. This is an administration that seeks to legislate when it is not in their purview, whether it be immigration, whether it be health care, or whether it now be a war that has been going on for 8 months without congressional authorization. This administration is in direct defiance of what Senator Obama ran on and what he was elected upon. He said no country should go to war without the authority of Congress unless under imminent attack. This is a great debate.

I signed the letter to Iran, but you know what? The message I was sending was to you. The message was to President Obama that we want you to obey the law. We want you to understand the separation of powers. If this agreement in any way modifies legislative sanctions, it will have to be passed by Congress. That is why I have supported Senator Corker's legislation that says exactly this. However, I have told Senator Corker privately I think that is the law anyway, that this will have to be passed. You cannot undo legislation.

So why did I sign this letter? I signed this letter because I signed it to an administration that does not listen, to an administration that at every turn tries to go around Congress because you think you cannot get your way. The President says, oh, the Congress will not do what I want, so I have got a pen and I have got my phone, and I am going to do what I want. The letter was to you. The letter was to Iran, but it should have been cc'd to the White House because the White House needs to understand that any agreement that removes or changes legislation will have to be passed by us.

Now, people can have different interpretations of things, but I will go through a couple of things that bother me about the AUMF. The AUMF in 2001 says that "nations or organizations that planned, authorized, committed, or aided in the attacks on 9/11" are the target. That is what the authorization is about. I do not read Boko Haram into that. I mean, if we are going to read Boko Haram into that, that is such a stretch that it is meaningless.

Senator Murphy talked about vagueness. It is pretty specific in 2001 what we were supposed to do. I was all in favor of that. We had to do what we had to do with Afghanistan, with those who attacked us. If we have to go other places, we should have authorizations. I am not saying I will not vote for the authorizations. We just need to have them.

So we have a new authorization that says we do not authorize enduring and offensive operations. The problem is it is so vague— I trust the military. When the military says this is not what we are contemplating, I trust you. But the thing is there will be another President who I may or may not trust, who may have a certain degree of lack of trust in this President saying that it is not being contemplated.

So we say it is not 697,000, but the next President could say it is, you know. Is it 100,000? You know, that would be my question, I guess, to Secretary Carter. We are saying it is not 697,000. Is it 100,000 troops, or could it be?

Secretary CARTER. Thank you, Senator. Well, it does not have a number in it, and that reflects the basic approach that this draft AUMF or proposed AUMF takes, which is to not attempt to enumerate or number, but to set a scope and a limit, a very meaningful limit——

Senator PAUL. But could it mean 100,000——

Secretary CARTER [continuing]. A meaningful limit referring to it, and the President specifically referred to the campaigns in Iraq and Afghanistan. And it just gets back to the whole logic of the campaign, which is to enable those in the region who can make a victory stick. That is the basic approach——

Senator PAUL. Right, and I understand not wanting—I understand not wanting to put a number on it. And when the authorization was passed in December, it did not put a number on it. It defined sort of the mission more precisely. In doing so, it basically defined what we are doing over there now. I see nothing that we are doing there now that would not have flown under the definition from December.

The problem is that without a geographic limit, we now have Boko Haram. People are saying it is sort of like, it is disdainful to say, well, you know, we want you all to pass something, but it does not really matter because we will just use 2001, which is just absurd. And it just means that Congress is inconsequential and so are the people in the country, that basically we will do what we want, and Boko Haram can be included under 2001. If Boko Haram is a threat to the country, bring it to me and we will vote, and I will listen honestly on whether we need to attack Boko Haram in Nigeria.

But the thing is that I understand how things change over time and how people transmute words to mean things that they really were not intended to mean. If 2001 can be applied to Boko Haram, I am very concerned about voting for this as it is worded because if we are going to go to war in Libya, I want to vote for war in Libya. If we are going to go to war in Nigeria, I want to vote for war in Nigeria. And I am not talking about an isolated small episode where we have to go knock out a cell of people that are organizing to attack us. You may be able to interpret that under the imminent attack sort of clause of the Constitution.

But I am concerned, that is why we get to numbers. Under this resolution, I believe you could have unlimited numbers of troops in Iraq. I understand you say it is not contemplated. I also believe you could have unlimited numbers of troops in Libya and in Nigeria, and now there are 30 nations that have pledged allegiance to ISIS. So words are important, and people worry about the danger of being too confining. We are not even anywhere close to that, because even when we thought we were confining in 2001, people have interpreted that to mean anything.

And so, really, I guess, Secretary Carter, do you understand that if it were to pass as it is now, there are those of us who would worry that this would be authorizing unlimited troops in 30 different nations if the administration saw fit to send them?

Secretary CARTER. Senator, I think that any AUMF, and certainly this proposed AUMF, tries to strike a balance between anticipating a wide enough range of contingencies that we can react in the way that we need to protect ourselves and that we anticipate the nature of this enemy, while being restrictive enough to suggest to not just the law, but to you and our force, the force for which I am responsible and General Dempsey is responsible, what we are contemplating here. We are trying to strike that balance.

It is always hard to strike a balance in language. I have said before I am not a lawyer. But in common sense terms, that is the balance that we are trying to strike. And I respect that different people might use different language to that effect, and I have learned enough in studying for this hearing about authorities for the use of military force to know that there are several avenues to do that. But I think that what is being done here is in recognition of a new chapter opening, namely the ISIL threat which opened last summer, the recognition that there is a new chapter in our effort to protect ourselves, and out of respect for that, a request for a specific authorization.

And I think—I understand that. I do not think that—I think the lawyers have said there is a legal necessity for it. It does not come from legal necessity. It comes from a recognition of a practical fact, which is something happened last summer, which created a new danger to which—the defeat of which we need to participate. We are not going to do it by ourselves. We are going to enable others to do it, and that is the principal insurance against it turning into an Iraq and Afghanistan. That is not what is needed here. That is not what will succeed here. So just speaking as the Secretary of Defense and, again, not a lawyer, it seems to me that is the logic that brought us here. And I understand it.

Senator PAUL. Thank you. And I just want to say I do not question your sincerity, and when you say it is not contemplated, I truly do believe you, that it is not contemplated. But I have to deal with words that 15 years from now I have to explain to my kids, and their friends, and their kids' kids, that something I voted for in 2015 still has us at war in 2030 in 30 different countries, okay?

It is an ongoing threat, but we need to keep the separation of powers. We need to vote on these things. And the reason it has to be precise is I cannot vote for something that is going to enable war in Libya, and Nigeria, and Yemen, and all these places with 100,000 troops. There has to be some kind of limitation. And it is not your sincerity I question. It is the politicians, and the next politician, and the next politician after you. But thank you very much.

The CHAIRMAN. Thank you. I have one followup question for Chairman Dempsey and Secretary Carter. I understand that Secretary Kerry has a hard stop, and if you felt like you wanted to miss my last question, I would not consider it rude, and would like for you to get on with your business if you need to do. If you want to stay, that would be fine.

Secretary KERRY. I really appreciate that. I do have a hard stop. Can I just take 1 minute for thing? I just wanted you to know that today the Treasury Department has authorized—has initiated additional sanctions on eight Ukrainian separatists, a Russian pro-separatist organization, three of its leaders, a Crimean bank, and additionally on some Yanukovych folks, supporters.

In addition to that, we are today providing immediately some $75 million of additional nonlethal assistance immediately to Ukraine in order to help them in nonlethal assistance. And as you know, other things are currently under consideration. But I just wanted you to be aware of that, Mr. Chairman.

The CHAIRMAN. Well, it is very timely. We thank you for that. We had a Ukraine-Russia hearing yesterday, and I know there is still the push to provide the lethal support. I know this—there were a lot of questions and some statements made today, but the fact is all of us deeply appreciate the tremendous amount of effort you put forth in your job. And we thank you for taking the time to be with us today with the many other demands that you have. Thank you.

If I could, gentlemen, Chairman Dempsey, if I could just follow up a little bit on the AUMF and the issue of being able to protect those that we train and equip against Assad's assaults, and the fact that it is your belief that the AUMF does not cover that, nor does the 2001 AUMF, and I assume Secretary Carter agrees with that assumption. Is that correct?

Secretary CARTER. I do. I do, yes. I am told separately just to get to your question, if the forces that we train and equip come under attack from Assad, would we have the legal authority to help them defend themselves. And my understanding of that question is that we do not foresee that happening any time soon, but a legal determination, I am told by the lawyers, has not been made whether we would have authority to do that or not. Again, I am not lawyer, but that is what I am told.

The CHAIRMAN. Yes, and I think that is what you may have said—someone said to Senator Graham last week. First of all, we thank you both for being here, and I know that coming before Senate panels is not first on your priority list in your current day jobs, but we appreciate the time here. So this is just really to tease this out a little bit.

It is a pretty big issue when you think about the fact that we have authorized the training and equipping, and that the administration apparently did talk some with you all. If I understand correctly, for there to be a clear legal determination, then that would mean that an additional authorization would need to be approved by Congress for you all to be able to protect, to train, and to equip folks against Assad.

That seems to me very problematic. I mean, you see the kind of consternation that takes place over the one that is now offered. To come back later with another one does not seem to me to be a particularly appropriate way to go about things. And so, Chairman Dempsey, what should be our thinking in that regard, and what is yours?

General DEMPSEY. First, Senator, I actually chuckled when you said how much we enjoy coming over here. But the truth is over the course of my 4 years as chairman, I have come to a deep appreciation of the fact that we do have an Article 1 responsibility to have these kind of conversations with you about our national security interests and the strategy to deliver them. So I actually want to thank you for running a very cordial hearing today on the topics.

As far as the—what are we going to do about protecting the new Syrian forces as they are fielded, that question is—I mentioned the term "active." We are in an active discussion. From the very beginning, though, we knew that we would come to the point where we had to make a decision about whether or not to protect them, and it was always my advice that we had to come to some conclusion to assure them that they would be protected. Now, the scope and scale of that protection is the part of this that is being actively debated. But the program will not succeed unless they believe themselves to have a reasonable chance of survival.

The CHAIRMAN. Let me just follow up, and, again, I appreciate the fact that you are not just looking at these issues in your role, but other issues in the Pacific and all around the world. And you have got to balance the resources that we have available to us. But back to that issue, can you understand why many of us here, knowing that getting Turkey involved in some way on the ground, probably matters some to our success over time? If we are going to continue on the policy path that we are on and the strategy, it is important.

So knowing that the President did not seek the authority to go against Assad—solely again, I am talking about not necessarily to take him on directly, but to be able to protect the train and equip personnel that will be reentering, and also to deal with some humanitarian issues and, let us face it, the Northwest Triangle right above Aleppo. That would give many of us, who certainly want to support this, some concern that there really is not a commitment level there to create, if you will, an effective ground effort. And I just wonder if you could respond to that a little bit.

General DEMPSEY. I cannot ease your concerns, but I can tell you that when I provide my military advice, it is key to the success of the new Syrian forces that they will have a degree of protection. And that, as Secretary Carter has said, is under active discussion.

The CHAIRMAN. Well, I assume then since that is key to success, those that are actually carrying out these activities would not be offended if Congress gave that authorization today.

General DEMPSEY. I leave that to you, our elected officials.

The CHAIRMAN. I wonder if Secretary Carter wants to respond to that, and I have one followup for you.

Secretary CARTER. Again, the practical answer to your very practical question is the one given by the chairman, namely that there can—there could be circumstances in which the forces that we train and equip come under attack from Assad's forces. And it is important to them or will be important to them to know whether and in what manner they will be supported. That is something under active discussion.

I do not believe that the legal aspect of that has been determined, so I cannot tell you. You would have to ask the White House counsel or our DOD counsel whether anything additional was required in the way of formal authorities to do that. I simply cannot answer that question for you. But I do think it is a very meaningful practical question, and I give the same answer to it that the chairman does.

The CHAIRMAN. And I will just—and I know that you all are in active discussion, and you have your own concerns, and those are not necessarily always addressed quickly, if you will, by those that make decisions in other places, and I understand that. I will say that from my perspective it does show a degree of lack of commitment from the White House that they would not go ahead on the front end, knowing that there is no way you can continue to recruit the folks that are involved in this train and equip program if they know they are going to come into the country and immediately be barrel bombed, and we are not going to support their efforts. It would be very difficult to recruit additional folks, as you have mentioned.

And it does cause me to be concerned about the administration's overall commitment if that is not being dealt with in this authorization when we have authorized the train and equip program several months ago. So this is just something I raise.

Secretary Carter, the reason for the question was the Persian Gulf war and the 600, almost 700,000 troops that were involved. To me, the enduring offensive ground combat language that was in the AUMF that was sent over would have allowed for that. It was a 7-month operation. That to me was not enduring—and very successful I might add. And so, you are saying that a 7-month operation from your standpoint would not qualify per the President's language? That would be too long.

Secretary CARTER. The reference you are using is to a campaign intended to destroy the military forces of another State. That is a fundamentally different kind of conflict from this one.

The CHAIRMAN. I got that.

Secretary CARTER. So the ability to compare them eludes me.

The CHAIRMAN. I understand you are making a difference there, and I understand the difference between going against a country and going against an entity like ISIS or Daesh. I guess what troubled me just a hair, and, again, we all respect deeply the way you have come in and taken charge. But talking about a seven-month operation being too long, that goes beyond, if you will, an enduring offensive. I just wish you would clarify that to some degree for the record. If it takes 2 or 3 years, I would assume you would not consider that to be enduring.

Secretary CARTER. What I have—I will just repeat what I said earlier about the time scale. We do not know how long it will take to defeat ISIL, and I explained earlier that I would not tell you that it was 3 years, which is the only duration included in this authorization of the use of military force. And it does not derive from any expectation of how long the campaign will last. It derives from the political calendar of our country.

So that is the time scale named and specified in the proposed AUMF, and that is its origin. And that is the only period of time that is specifically named in the AUMF, and that is its derivation.

The CHAIRMAN. I know that Senator Menendez indicated he did not have any questions. Okay, go ahead.

Senator MENENDEZ. I do not have any questions, Mr. Chairman. I just have a comment. First of all, I want to share with—along with what, I think, every member of this committee and of the Senate, our thoughts and prayers are with these service members who were lost. This underlines that there is risk once you don the uniform, even if you are not under enemy fire. And so, our thoughts and prayers are with the families.

Also it reminds me as someone who did not vote for the process of sequester that we cannot ask you to do everything we ask you to do if we do not find relief from sequester here along the way. We seem to somehow ignore that, but I do not think both of you have that luxury. We have to deal with that.

Finally, I do hope that we can get to a point to find the right balance, and that is not easy in this proposition, to give you an AUMF that gives you the wherewithal to degrade and defeat ISIL, but by the same token does not provide an open-ended check. And I think that the real concern here is for some of us who lived under shock and awe and were told Iraqi oil was going to pay for everything, and so a lot of lives and national treasure were spent, that even well-intentioned efforts can move in a totally different direction.

And this is the most critical vote that any Member of the Congress will take, which is basically a vote on war and peace and life and death. And so, for those of us who have been pursuing this to try to find the right spot, the one thing I want you to take away from the hearing is that I do not think there is a Democrat or Republican who does not believe that we have to degrade or defeat ISIL. We stand collectively with you.

And as we struggle to get to the right wording with the right authorization, I just hope you can go back to the men and women who served this country with great sacrifice, and in that spirit we are united. And so, our only cause here is to find out how is the best way to ensure that and at the end not ensure, you know, an endless war, which is the concern of many.

Secretary CARTER. Thank you for saying that. It means a lot.

Senator MENENDEZ. Thank you both.

The CHAIRMAN. Thank you. I was just handed a note just as I think you all were a minute ago. I just want to end—my last statement before thanking you by saying it is my understanding the DOD senior lawyers are sitting behind you. And it is my understanding as we leave here that the authorization that has been put before us and the 2001 authorization—neither one give clear cut authority for you all to be able to defend the train and equip program against Assad's assaults. I just want to state that. I do not think anybody is disagreeing with that. Is that correct?

Secretary CARTER. That is my understanding, and I would be happy to have our legal team speak to you about that. That is my understanding, Senator.

The CHAIRMAN. Well, since I do not see them waving their hands back there, I am assuming they are speaking now. So I would just like to close also by telling you how much we respect you both and how much we appreciate your service to your country, how much we appreciate you taking the time to come up here. I think this has been very helpful to all of us. We wish you well.

And the record will be open until the close of business Friday. I hope if questions come, you will answer them as promptly as possible.

The CHAIRMAN. Again, thank you for your service and for being here today. The meeting is adjourned.

Secretary CARTER. Thank you, Mr. Chairman.

[Whereupon, at 12:40 p.m., the hearing was adjourned.]

ADDITIONAL MATERIAL SUBMITTED FOR THE RECORD

PREPARED STATEMENT OF SENATOR BARBARA BOXER

Chairman Corker, Senator Menendez—thank you for holding this important hearing today.

I would also like to thank our panel of distinguished witnesses for appearing before the committee and for their service to our country.

This hearing will focus on the most difficult and somber responsibility of this committee—authorizing the use of military force.

Committing American service men and women to fight in a conflict overseas is not a decision I take lightly. That is why I have deep reservations about President Obama's proposed authorization for the use of military force—or AUMF—against the Islamic State of Iraq and the Levant (ISIL), which he submitted to Congress last month.

I fear that the President's proposal leaves open the door for American combat troops to be sent to fight another ground war in the Middle East.

The restriction on "enduring offensive ground combat operations" is no restriction at all. The language is vague, confusing, and overly broad. And it gives this President and the next one the sole discretion to interpret the phrase as they see fit.

In fact, the Congressional Research Service (CRS) came to this same conclusion in a legal brief completed at my request. In the brief, CRS states that, "It seems doubtful that a limitation on 'enduring offensive ground combat operations' would present sufficient judicially manageable standards by which a court could resolve any conflict that might arise between Congress and the executive branch over the interpretation of the phrase or its application to U.S. involvement in hostilities."

I cannot and will not support such an AUMF.

If we have learned anything over the last decade, it is that we cannot commit tens of thousands of American service men and women to another open-ended ground conflict in the Middle East.

This is the commitment President Obama reiterated in his State of the Union Address, saying: "Instead of getting dragged into another ground war in the Middle East, we are leading a broad coalition, including Arab nations, to degrade and ultimately destroy this terrorist group."

I believe that an AUMF against ISIL should better reflect the President's promise and the strategy he has laid out to the American people to work with a broad international coalition to confront these ruthless terrorists.

As Congress works to debate and craft a new AUMF, I hope we will revisit the AUMF that passed out of this committee in December under the leadership of Senator Menendez. I voted for that AUMF because it supported the President's strategy of building a broad coalition to combat ISIL and reflected his commitment that American combat troops would not be sent back to the Middle East to fight another ground war.

We must learn from the tragic foreign policy mistakes of the past. We cannot afford to make them again.

———

RESPONSES OF SECRETARY OF DEFENSE ASHTON CARTER TO QUESTIONS SUBMITTED BY SENATOR BOB CORKER

ASSESSMENT OF ISIS STRATEGY

Question. What is your assessment of the effectiveness of the military and political strategy against ISIS?

Answer. Militarily, the administration's counter-Islamic State in Iraq and Syria (ISIS) strategy is making progress. U.S. and coalition airstrikes are taking out ISIS's command and control, supply lines, fighters, and their military and economic infrastructure. The airstrikes have debilitated ISIS's oil producing, processing, and transportation infrastructure.

There have been some successes on the ground in Iraq, where some organized forces—Iraq security forces or peshmerga—worked in coordination with the coalition and reclaimed areas once controlled by ISIS. Efforts to train and advise Iraq security forces are ongoing at four sites across Iraq, with cooperation from our coalition partners. There has also been some slow progress by the Government of Iraq (GOI) to integrate Sunni tribal forces in Anbar province into the Iraq Security Forces. The coalition is committed to continue working with both the GOI and the tribes to facilitate this integration of forces.

Military means, however, will not be sufficient to counter ISIS. Iraq will be stable and secure only when it has a stable and inclusive government that addresses the needs of Iraq's diverse society. Prime Minister Abadi has taken steps to demonstrate his commitment to reconciliation and inclusive governance, but I refer you to the State Department for a more detailed assessment of the GOI's political progress.

The situation is more complex in Syria due to the absence of a national military or civilian partner, and the lack of a cohesive opposition. Nonetheless, there has been success in Kobani, where a combination of airstrikes and local defenders forced ISIS to withdraw from the area. This is why the effort to train and equip appropriately vetted Syrian opposition forces to counter ISIS is so essential.

However, to stop the conflict that has fuelled the rise of ISIS, there must ultimately be a political solution in Syria. This will take time and perseverance.

AUTHORITY AND RESOURCES

Question. Do you feel you have the authority and resources today to achieve the goal of defeating ISIS both in Syria and Iraq?

Answer. Yes. The National Defense Authorization Act (NDAA) for Fiscal Year (FY) 2015 and the DOD Appropriations Act, 2015, provide authority and funding for ongoing operations in support of Operation Inherent Resolve. The Iraq Train and Equip Fund, authorized by the NDAA for FY 2015, provides the authority and resources to train and equip Iraq security forces, including Kurdish and Sunni tribal forces. These statutes also enable a parallel effort against the Islamic State in Iraq and Syria (ISIS) in Syria, authorizing and funding a program to train and equip appropriately vetted Syrian opposition forces.

It is my belief that the 2001 Authorization for the Use of Military Force (AUMF) provides adequate legal authority to use U.S. military force against ISIS in both Iraq and Syria. I also believe that the 2002 Iraq AUMF provides legal authority for military operations against ISIS in Iraq and, in some circumstances, against ISIS in Syria.

It is also my belief that the President's proposed ISIS-specific AUMF would give the Department the flexibility it needs to carry out the military campaign against ISIS, and would send a strong signal to our military, our coalition partners, and our adversaries that the United States is united in its effort to destroy ISIS.

The Department's efforts have degraded ISIS, but the defeat of ISIS in Iraq and Syria will depend not only on the Department's continuing efforts, but also on political solutions both in Iraq and Syria.

TITLE 10 TRAIN AND EQUIP PROGRAM

Question. Do you anticipate forces trained under the Title 10 Train and Equip program to one day fight Assad?

Answer. The intent and focus of our Train and Equip program is to prepare appropriately vetted Syrian opposition forces to fight against the Islamic State in Iraq and Syria (ISIS). I recognize, though, that many of these groups now fight on two or three fronts, including against ISIS, other violent extremists, and the Syrian Government. The administration has always said that Assad must go as he has lost the legitimacy to lead, and that a political solution is necessary to end the war and stop the chaos that has fuelled the rise of ISIS.

RESPONSE OF GEN MARTIN DEMPSEY TO QUESTION
SUBMITTED BY SENATOR BOB CORKER

BEST MILITARY ADVICE

Question. Are U.S. forces today conducting operations in the fight against ISIS that are in line with your best military advice for achieving the administration's stated goals?

Answer. Yes, operations involving U.S. forces are in line with my best military advice. In Iraq, the coalition is conducting operations that enable Iraqi forces to conduct offensive operations against ISIL. In recent months the coalition has blunted ISIL's momentum in Iraq, trained and equipped Iraqis and enabled Iraqis to retake lost terrain from ISIL. I believe the Government of Iraq must own this fight. We cannot do it for them—but we can help them to be successful. That is what our campaign plan in Iraq is designed to do.

In Syria we continue to degrade ISIL through our air campaign and have made significant progress with our coalition partners in setting the stage for the train and equip program. Our comprehensive effort in both Iraq and Syria continues to depend upon a strong network of partnerships.

○

www.ingramcontent.com/pod-product-compliance
Lightning Source LLC
Chambersburg PA
CBHW081858280526
45789CB00007B/2751